Night
of the
Twisters

Night
of the
Twisters

by Ivy Ruckman

THOMAS Y. CROWELL
New York

NIGHT OF THE TWISTERS

Copyright © 1984 by Ivy Ruckman

All rights reserved. No part of this book may be used or reproduced in any manner whatsoever without written permission except in the case of brief quotations embodied in critical articles and reviews. Printed in the United States of America. For information address Thomas Y. Crowell Junior Books, 10 East 53rd Street, New York, N.Y. 10022. Published simultaneously in Canada by Fitzhenry & Whiteside Limited, Toronto.

Designed by Joyce Hopkins

1 2 3 4 5 6 7 8 9 10

First Edition

Library of Congress Cataloging in Publication Data
Ruckman, Ivy.
  Night of the twisters.

  Summary: A fictional account of the night freakish and devastating tornadoes hit Grand Island, Nebraska, as experienced by a twelve-year-old, his family, and friends.
  1. Children's stories, American. 2. Grand Island (Neb.)—Tornado, 1980—Juvenile fiction. [1. Grand Island (Neb.)—Tornado, 1980. 2. Tornadoes—Fiction] I. Title.
PZ7.R844Ni 1984   [Fic]   83-46168
ISBN 0-690-04408-9
ISBN 0-690-04409-7 (lib. bdg.)

For Cindy, Mark, and Ryan, who made it,
and for Tia, who didn't

Grand Island, Neb., June 4 (AP)—A string of seven tornadoes devastated this central Nebraska city last night, killing four persons and injuring 134.

Initial reports said five persons were killed, and one county official said this morning that she thought more than 30 bodies had been found. . . .

The city was battered by the tornadoes over a three-hour period. When they were over, a six-block-wide swath along Grand Island's two main streets was devastated.

The Federal Emergency Management Administration said that 513 homes and 60 businesses had been destroyed. In addition, 450 homes and 15 businesses were damaged. . . .

Radar indicated that the tornadoes that hit Grand Island were touched off by a thunderstorm cell at least 35 miles wide that formed shortly before 8 P.M.

Associated Press, June 4, 1980

As Told by
Dan Hatch

When I was a little kid, I thought a red-letter day was when you got a red letter in the mailbox. Pretty dumb, huh? It finally dawned on me that a red-letter day is when something terrific and wonderful happens to you. Usually something unexpected.

Take that April Saturday when I won five hundred dollars in cash and merchandise. Now *that* was a red-letter day if I ever saw one! But who'd have guessed? A plain, open space on the calendar, that day started out just like any other, with Frosty Flakes for breakfast and Mom posting my jobs on the kitchen corkboard. "Don't forget to change the kitty litter, Dan," she said, just as she had every Saturday for as long as I could remember.

By noon of April 19, I had entered the Dairy Queen Bike Race because my best friend, Arthur, dared me. By two o'clock I was crossing the finish line seventy-ninth, with only two cyclists behind me. Who'd have guessed a beginner like me would win the racers' raffle afterward?

Besides the one hundred dollars from Grand Island Thrift and Loan, I won a slick new racing bike (Schwinn Voyageur, 26 lbs., with Diacompe 500 G sidepull brakes and a jet-black frame). The prize also included a racing helmet, an aluminum bike pump, and three packages of Fruit-of-the-Loom underwear, which I gave to Arthur because he wears a men's small.

Now that's the kind of day that ought to have a tag on it. It could read:

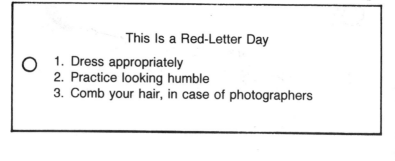

This Is a Red-Letter Day
1. Dress appropriately
2. Practice looking humble
3. Comb your hair, in case of photographers

Now that I'm older and more experienced, I know there are black-letter days as well as red-letter ones. Those BIGGEES, the real blockbusters that mess up your life, aren't marked on the calendar, either. You never know ahead of time when you're getting one of those. If I had my way—if I were in charge of the world, as Dad sometimes says—the black-letter days would be announced, for sure.

I've thought about this a lot. What if God or someone actually did send out doomsday letters via the postal service? Wouldn't that be something? Say you wake up to a nice, regular day. Everybody's in a good mood, a perfumy breeze is swinging in from the south. La-de-da! Then you go out to bring in the mail.

"What's this?" you gasp, staring at a black envelope in your hands.

You rip it open, trembling all the way to the elbows.

"Furnace explosion planned," it says, "two o'clock today."

Or maybe "Head-on collision with a Peterbilt truck. Washington and Fourth Street."

Or . . . "Tornado on Tuesday!"

If people got notices like that in advance, it would save a lot of trouble and grief. It's those black surprises that get to you, those things people call acts of God because they have to blame someone.

My all-time worst black-letter day was June 3 of last summer. There were no notices mailed out on that occasion, for sure. There were no indications at all.

"Twenty percent probability of thunderstorms toward evening" was what the local weatherman said that morning.

"So what's new?" Mom talked back to him, poking another spoonful of cereal in my baby brother's smiling mouth.

To tell you the truth, the weather was the last thing on my mind. Arthur and I had big plans for that Tuesday. Crafts class first, at my Aunt Goldie's place. A couple of hot burritos at Taco John's after. Later, a bike hike out to the Platte River and a swim at Mormon Island. According to my Grandpa Hatch, the best swimming in south-central Nebraska exists right there, where the big island separates the Platte. With school out for good, Arthur and I were planning to get in on some of it.

Unless you count the long cirrus clouds strung across the morning sky as Arthur and I pedaled off to Aunt Goldie's, there were no warnings at all that day in June. None.

Five O'clock

Arthur and I rolled over on our backs on the warm sandy beach at Mormon Island State Park. We'd just had our first swim of the summer, and now it was nearing five o'clock.

"You plan to keep going to that crafts class?" Arthur asked, putting his hands beneath his head and gazing up at the sky.

Now I ought to mention right here at the beginning that my friend Arthur is no ordinary human being. He's smart. He studies things. As Arthur himself says, he cogitates. I could tell by the way he was squinting into the sun that he was thinking hard about something.

Miss Stevens, our social studies teacher, pointed out in class one day: "Arthur," she said, standing between him and the window, "you just have to be the Original Gazer. Tell me, honestly now, what are you pining for *out there* that you don't have *in here*?"

"Freedom," he said. Not sassy-like or anything, just stating the facts.

Now, lying next to me, he was outlining cloud patterns with his big toe while he gazed. I raised myself on one elbow.

"Don't you like crafts class?" I asked.

"Not much."

I poked finger holes in the sand. "Heck, maybe Aunt Goldie had a stomachache today."

"Ha!"

"Maybe she swallowed a prune."

"Including the pit?"

"Pit, too," I said, "and the hairy green worm curled up next to it. That would give her an awesome bellyache."

"I've never heard of a prune worm."

I rolled back onto the sand. Arthur would probably go home and look up prune worms. He has books on everything—birds, trees, flowers, insects, amphibians, prunes.

" 'Bring some Indian crafts ideas when you come,' " Arthur said, mimicking my Aunt Goldie. "So I took my idea. She hated it."

"Aw, she was thinking of basket weaving or pottery painting. You know—something regular and *Indiany*. She'd never even heard of a bull-roarer."

"She thought I made it up. It's a toy Indian kids used to make, for crying out loud. That thing is authentic! If I'd called it a thunderstick instead of a bull-roarer, maybe she'd have—"

"I guess you shouldn't have demonstrated it. You know . . . right there in her basement under that electric light bulb. . . ." I circled my wrist overhead, winding up like some cham*peen* calf roper. Then I broke out laughing all over again. Once Arthur got to swinging that bull-roarer around his head, once it started whizzing and roaring like a whirlwind, we couldn't hear anything else. Until the sheared-off light bulb landed on the Ping-Pong table, that is.

"Shut up!" Arthur ordered.

I controlled myself. I didn't want big old Arthur to sit on me, the way he does when he gets mad.

9

(He's not gross, you understand, but he could live on his own fat cells for a month if he had to. Of course, he thinks of that as an advantage.)

Suddenly the sun, which had slid out for swimming earlier, disappeared behind the clouds again. This time it looked gone for good. I watched an army of goose bumps rise on my bare belly and thought about starting home.

Squinty-eyed, Arthur was still climbing the stair steps of a mighty thunderhead with his big toe. I knew he wasn't through brooding about what had happened that morning.

"If she makes us do rain dances, I'm quitting," he said.

"Oh, you know my Aunt Goldie. She's such a flake! She forgets half of what she says. Now that everybody wants to make bull-roarers and nobody wants to decorate pots and stuff, I bet she'll give up on Indian crafts."

Goldie, who teaches at the Riverside Dance Studio, also happens to be my mom's younger sister. Because she's divorced and has a hard time supporting herself, I get stuck having to enroll in her personal fulfillment classes every summer.

"It's the least we can do," Mom says, laying out her case each spring when Aunt Goldie drops off her hundreds of fliers for me to deliver. (On my own time. Without pay.)

So far, she's taught Arthur and me how to play Hacky Sack, tennis, backgammon, and boring bridge. Last summer we took boys' ballet in her basement while a class of mothers upstairs did aerobic dancing. When Aunt Goldie twisted her knee demonstrating an exercise position for us, she substituted Dungeons and Dragons for the remainder of our ballet lessons. That suited Arthur and me just fine.

"Let's go," I said suddenly, beginning to shiver. Though the day had been warm and muggy, the weather was changing fast.

Arthur sat up and reached for his jeans. I did the same.

Little groups along the beach were breaking up, too. Mothers were shaking out towels, yelling for their kids to hurry.

We finished dressing, but not before I spotted Stacey and Ronnie Vae coming toward us across the sand.

"Holy cow!" I muttered. Quickly I turned my back on them. There's nothing I hate more than zipping up my pants in front of a girl.

Arthur chortled as he zipped his up right there

in plain sight. He has six sisters, so what does he care? In fact, beautiful fourteen-year-old Stacey and ten-year-old Ronnie Vae are two of them.

"I didn't know you guys were here," Stacey said, tossing her long black hair and treating me to a flash of dimples. She knows I have a crush on her, has known it ever since I told Arthur and swore him to secrecy. "Where were you guys swimming, anyway?" she asked.

Arthur pointed off to where the Platte River ambles through the state park. "We've got this private spot over there with a lot of water snakes—"

"Liar!" Stacey cut him off.

I glanced Ronnie's way as I knelt to tie my sneakers. She was covered with goose bumps, same as me. Of course, I have enough muscle to keep me warm, but she's so skinny. I imagine it must be embarrassing for her to walk around in a bathing suit, looking the way she does.

"Why don't you two ride us to the Conoco station so I can call Mom?" Stacey asked, her eyes on me and my bike. "We want to get home before it rains."

"What do you care?" Arthur said. "You're already wet."

"You'll ride me double, won't you, Dan?"

I grinned. I was Silly Putty in her hands.

"Well, I'm not waiting around!" Ronnie Vae said as she marched off.

Stacey's older than Arthur and me by two years, so she's used to getting her own way. She wasn't about to give up.

"*Please?*" she kept on. "I've never been on your new bike."

"Look, Eustacia Marie," Arthur sneered, using her revolting given name, "Dan can give you a lift if he's dumb enough to, but I'm not riding Ronnie Vae anywhere!"

So we wheeled our bikes up to the road, with Stacey walking between us. I was longing to have her hanging on to my waist while I demonstrated my biceps and quadriceps and my great cycling skills, but I lost out. When Stacey's loyalty to her underfed sister got the best of her, she ran off, yelling for Ronnie to wait up.

Clouds were building fast as we started pedaling for home. The way the wind was whipping those trees around at the state park should have clued me that something big was on the way, but I wasn't worried then. I figured we were in for more rain. Maybe a hailstorm, too, if the greenish look of the sky meant anything.

Suddenly I realized I was hungry as a bear out of hibernation.

"Want to eat at my house?" I called to Arthur over my shoulder.

"What are you having?"

"How should I know?"

Our voices trailed off in the wind, so we didn't talk much after that. We had a long way to go, and the pumping took all our breath.

Thirty or so minutes later we were cutting across the huge cement parking area that surrounds the Fonner Park Racetrack. That's where we always sprint on our bikes, but the wind was so strong it made speed impossible.

Finally, as I was turning the corner onto Sand Crane Drive, a comics page from a newspaper hit my front spokes and immediately got itself shredded. I squeezed my hand brakes and stopped. I couldn't believe what I was seeing—a whole ton of newsprint was scattered up and down my street. It looked as if the Grand Island *Daily Independent* had set out to toilet paper the entire neighborhood.

I rested a minute, waiting for Arthur to catch up so we could laugh about it together. As I waited, I wiped my face on my damp T-shirt and read *Peanuts.*

Isn't it funny how you remember all the crummy little details on one of those black-letter days? My folks say it was that way with them the day President Kennedy was shot way back in 1963. And Belle Smiley, the oldest person in our neighborhood, said she could still remember exactly where she was and what she was thinking on Pearl Harbor Day.

"I was standing right there inside that screen door," she told me once, after inviting me in for cookies. "I was watching a box elder bug crawl across the outside of the screen. I was just standing there, daring that bug to stick his head through a hole we had in the screen. That's when the paperboy came by hollering 'Extra! Extra! Attack on Pearl Harbor!'

"I didn't move. I just stood there, tears running down my cheeks. I knew my boys would be going off to war . . . and I knew they mightn't come back." Belle Smiley went on telling me about Pearl Harbor through four more cookies and a second glass of milk. I swear, I learned more about history from her than I did in school.

Anyway, I can remember everything about that Tuesday, too. Every little detail.

I remember the bottom-heavy look of the sky and those strong blasts of air that hit us going home. I remember thinking about the girls and being sorry we hadn't given them a lift. It never did get around to raining steady, but the on-and-off-again rain squalls made you think it would. If Ronnie's goose bumps were any indication, the poor girl's bones would be clanking by the time she and Stacey got to that Conoco station to phone their mom.

I can even tell you what we had for supper on that June the third. All I have to do to recall the wonderful smell of our kitchen that night is to close my eyes and inhale. Mom had just taken a chocolate meringue pie out of the oven.

Six O'clock

"Set the table, Danny," Mom said as soon as we walked in. "Your dad has to eat and run tonight."

"Okay!"

I detoured Arthur toward the bathroom so we could wash.

"Is that chocolate pudding or chocolate pie?" he asked, sniffing the air. He can identify a dessert faster than my Grandpa Hatch, who I used to think held the world's record.

We took turns lathering our hands, squeezing the bar of soap back and forth to each other, laughing.

Back in the kitchen, I was relieved to see that my brother Ryan's high chair was empty. I loved it when he was napping.

"Where's Ryan?" I asked anyway.

Mom was opening a bag of wiener buns. She looked tiredly across the room at Arthur, who was leaning in the doorway watching me count out plates.

"Hi there, Arthur," she said, blowing hair out of her eyes. "Baby's cutting teeth, Danny. Took all afternoon for him to fall asleep."

I could smell the pork and beans and could hear it bubbling on the stove. Beans and wieners were our standard supper when Ryan was fussy.

"Can Arthur eat with us?" I asked.

"If he calls his mother," she said matter-of-factly.

Before Ryan was born, Mom used to call Arthur and me her twins, meaning my buddy and I were practically inseparable. Of course, Arthur has dark skin and a mop of wavy black hair, whereas I'm one of those yellow-haired, freckle-faced types. He's short and fat; I'm not. We could never pass for brothers, let alone twins, because we're different in other ways, too. He's a thinker; I'm a doer. He's crazy about books; I go bonkers over bikes. Just the same, we consider ourselves blood relatives, and that's what counts.

As Arthur stepped to the wall phone and dialed, Mom gave me a sideways look that meant *Why don't you clear things with me first?*

I just lifted an extra glass and plate off the shelf and pretended not to notice.

To tell you the truth, I halfway felt sorry for Mom right then. I remembered how jolly she used to be— before Ryan was born. Last year, when she was working, she dressed up every day in her beauty salon uniform, her shiny brown hair in this wedge cut that Dad liked so much. Now her hair was kind of stringy and her nerves were frazzled. She claimed to be perfectly content staying home with her baby and her sewing machine, but I wasn't convinced. I overheard something she said to Dad one night when they were getting ready for bed. "I miss *me*," she said, sounding so lonesome for her old self it made me sad.

I frowned as I laid out four forks on four napkins. We'd been one small happy family for eleven great years: John Hatch, Linda Hatch, and me, Dan. As far as I was concerned, we could have gone on that way forever—without Ryan.

19

"What are we having tonight?" Arthur asked into the phone.

"Potato salad?" He made a face. "Mrs. Hatch asked if I could eat over here. Can I? Yeah . . . honest." Long pause. His mouth went dismal on one side as he held the phone out toward Mom. "She wants to talk to *you*."

"Stir the beans, Danny," Mom said. "Hello, Karen, what's up? Yes, I asked him . . . more or less." She grinned. "You know how it goes, wherever they light first. Yes, I'm sure. John's going to be leaving, anyway. He's helping his father on the farm tonight." She listened awhile. "Yes, we were out on the place last week, too, taking down storm windows. Mother Hatch has a fit if she doesn't get her fresh air."

"Ask if Arthur can stay and watch TV after," I whispered, feeling Mom's biceps in the arm that held up the phone. *Not bad*, I thought. She had said lugging the baby around was getting her in shape.

"Hey, feel her muscles," I invited Arthur, still whispering, but he wouldn't.

Mom hung up.

"Why didn't you ask—" I began.

"Danny," she cut me off, "will you not be so rude when I'm on the phone?"

Then Ryan started crying, and Mom's face looked

the way I felt, having just been scolded.

"Throw two extra wieners in the pan," she said as she headed for Ryan's room, which had once been my room, before the bunny wallpaper and the rocking chair. I got moved into the "den," as Mom still calls the extra bedroom when she forgets.

I took the package of wieners out of the fridge and added three to be on the safe side. At a baseball game Arthur can eat four hot dogs and still have room for an order of Nachos.

We'd hardly got the TV going when my dad walked in the back door. I heard him sling his John Deere hat on the wall peg, heard his booming voice next. "Don't tell me that Darlington kid's here again!"

I poked Arthur, who smiled happily. He knows how much my dad loves to tease.

However, Dad wasn't teasing a few minutes later when he raised me up off the floor by one arm.

"Is that your brand-new racing bike lying out there in the weather?" he asked me, nose to nose.

He let me drop to the floor from that great height, but the quiz continued. "You boys know what baseball-size hail can do to a bicycle?"

He marched on to the bathroom as Arthur and I got up, exchanging eyebrows.

"No . . . what?" Arthur had to ask.

"Ever see what a meat mallet does to a tough steak?"

I hate it when people answer questions with questions, but he got his point across.

"That bad, huh?" Arthur muttered as we went outside to put my bike in the garage. Arthur's bike was already so hashed, we left it on the grass where it was.

Later, during supper, with my baby brother fussing and spitting applesauce all over, I remembered how nice and peaceful meals were six months ago. Even our cat, Minerva, couldn't be in the house at mealtimes anymore, not since we caught her licking egg off the baby's face.

The worst part was, any good news I'd saved for suppertime seemed to rank second to whatever cutesy sound Ryan was experimenting with at the time.

"Blug," Ryan would say, bubbling and drooling. Every time, Dad's head would swivel like a machine—away from me and toward him. And the slightest little "unnnnh" he made before cutting loose with an ear-splitting scream would get Mom straight to her feet.

Now, having finished his quota of hot dogs, even

Arthur was making eyes at my brother. "Gitsy, gitsy," he cooed, walking across Ryan's undershirt with his fingers. Ryan rewarded him with a silly smile.

Used to be, we had conversation at the supper table.

"Well, Danny, what'd you do at school?" Dad would ask, buttering a roll or something.

I'd tell him and he'd listen. He'd laugh or shake his head or make a joke about what I'd said. Mom might get in on it, or she might just sit there, waiting her turn. In those days she was doing hair at Carol's Boutique, so she had lots of stuff to tell every night.

If Arthur happened to be eating with us, Dad would include him, too.

"Go over your sisters' names again, Wart," he might say, as he had off and on for the two years Arthur had lived in Grand Island. "I think I've nearly got 'em straight now. One more time ought to do it."

Then Arthur would recite and Mom would try not to giggle.

"Eustacia Marie," he'd begin, his brown eyes serious as anything, "Veronica Vae . . . Gwyneth Elaine . . . Tabitha Tess . . . Theodosia Désirée . . . and the baby, Angélique. Angélique's the last. She doesn't have a middle name because Mama's going to add it later when she gets to wanting another baby."

I swear, it was like listening to Genesis-Exodus-Leviticus at Sunday school!

Every time, Arthur recited them deadpan. And every time, Dad cocked his head to one side, pretending to memorize the names. His mustache would twitch, and I'd know he was holding back on his loud "haw-haws." Sometimes, on request, Arthur would also recite the titles of the paperback novels the names came from. The list was funniest to Mom, who had read half of them. She and Mrs. Darlington loved trading books.

Ah yes, I thought, stabbing the last bean on my plate: *The Hatch Family, B.R.*

Mom handed Arthur and me our wedges of chocolate pie just before Ryan started in again with his stiff-legged screaming.

"Have you tried rubbing his gums with paregoric?" Dad asked Mom, all concerned.

"I may have to if I want to get Mother Hatch's dress finished tonight."

Mom took Ryan onto her lap and let him suck on a piece of ice.

"Are you still going out to the farm tonight?" I asked once I got the chance.

"I have to, Danny. The tractor quit two days ago. The mechanic there in Phillips can't get to it before Friday, and your grandfather has to put in his crop of milo."

Then Dad was up, pushing back his chair and kissing Mom. He rubbed Ryan's fuzzy head and gave my neck a squeeze before he took off.

"I'll have dessert later," he said. "Dad's expecting me before dark so we can tow that sucker into the shed."

He slapped on his cap, then headed for the bathroom to put his green coveralls back on.

My dad's a mechanic. He loves getting his hands into greasy old engines and making them purr again. In fact, Dad's pride and joy, a rare white 1953 Corvette, stood engine-stripped in our garage that night, waiting for new main bearings. I knew for a fact Dad would rather have been working on his 'Vette than fixing that bucket of bolts Grandpa calls a tractor, but my father is also a good son. I've heard Grandpa tell him so a dozen times.

On his way out of the house Dad yelled at me to do the dishes for Mom.

"But Arthur's here . . ." I hollered back, remembering that Arthur never worked when he had company at his house.

"All the more reason to help," Dad answered.

I groaned, but it came out sounding worse than I meant it to. Dad was back in the kitchen in no time.

"Listen, young man, your mother hasn't had a minute's rest all day. You do the dishes and anything else she wants you to, you hear?" His finger poked a hole in my shoulder. "It wouldn't hurt you to baby-sit your brother once in a while, either."

He let the back door slam behind him, but I could still hear what he said as he got in the pickup: "The sun doesn't rise and set on you!"

Seven O'clock

Arthur helped me do dishes *and* fold diapers that night. He didn't seem to mind. In fact, once he caught on to Mom's quick-flip system, his diaper pile grew faster than mine.

Mostly, we didn't talk while we worked. I think Arthur knew I was feeling bad. I couldn't forget what Dad had said, no matter how hard I tried to turn my mind to Stacey or something pleasant. I kept hearing him say, "The sun doesn't rise and set on you!" Accent the *you*.

The truth is, I'd never once thought the sun rose and set on me, so why would he say that?

I shook my head and carried the folded diapers down the hall to Ryan's room. Mom was rocking him to sleep, but she smiled at me—and winked—as if she knew how bad I felt.

A little later, while Arthur and I were trying to decide if we wanted to ride bikes or hang around waiting for *Happy Days* on TV, Aunt Goldie popped in at the kitchen door. She was wearing pink shorts and a frilly blouse, carrying a coffee can full of strawberries.

"Hi, guys," she greeted us. She held up the can before setting it in the sink. "From Mrs. Smiley's garden," she explained. "Where's your Mom, D.J.?" (That's short for Daniel John.)

"She's getting Ryan to sleep. He's been a terror all day."

"Oh, no," she said, making a face. Then she bent down and hugged me. "It's not always easy having a baby in the house, is it?"

I was glad somebody understood.

She peeked down the hall but came right back, her finger to her lips. "I'd better not disturb them. Linda would kill me."

Now, I love my aunt and all that, but I didn't want

to get stuck having to sit there and talk to her while Mom was busy with Ryan. I made a quick decision and got to my feet.

"Arthur and I were just leaving to ride bikes."

"Hey, wait—tell you what—I just stopped by to borrow Linda's bowling ball. Riverside's league starts tonight. And in case I can make myself go . . ." She rolled her eyes. "You know where she keeps it?"

"You going to Westside Lanes or Meves?" Arthur asked my aunt. I headed for the hall closet.

"Meves," she said, "but only if I can't get out of it. I mean . . . I'm a dancer, you know? It's just not my thing. I'd almost rather stay home and straighten my hair."

It was a family joke: blond curly-top Goldie staying home to straighten her hair. She was always getting suckered in on something she didn't want to do.

Aunt Goldie thanked me for the bowling ball and left the house when we did, but not before kissing me on top of the head.

"Be careful or the wind'll blow you over," she warned as she got in her car and backed out.

I could see what she meant once we hit the street. Even riding my slick new Voyageur, head down, in first gear, it was tough going. Arthur—on his dented-up, rusted-out, untuned BMX—was practically standing still.

"Let's go over to your house," I shouted, thinking of Stacey.

"Why?"

"I don't know."

I sped up so I could test my brakes. Arthur popped a wheelie, then squeaked to a halt alongside me. He tried spitting into the wind, but it splattered over the curb two yards behind us. Some breeze!

"Bet I could stay all night with you," he said in the sly way he has of inviting himself.

"Why don't you, then?"

"Mom says I shouldn't be the one to bring it up."

"Okay, so I'll bring it up. Would you sleep over, *pu-leeze*?"

Arthur's face brightened. I guess mine did, too, because we took off pumping hard and laughing for no reason at all. On wheels again, I was definitely feeling better.

We'd nearly covered the three blocks between my house and his when the streetlights came on. With the sky all black and snarly with thunder the way it was, lights were popping on inside houses, too. Made them look like friendly little way stations in the dusk.

I swung around at the corner of Fonda Way and waited for Arthur, who was still grunting and puffing half a block away.

I'll always be glad I took time to notice how beautiful Sand Crane Drive looked in that weird half-light. Up and down the street trees swayed in unison, like dancers in a chorus line. Overhead, clouds boiled so low you could almost jump up and grab them. It was unreal, all the creaking and moaning going on.

Arthur went on past me, peeling left on Fonda Way when he should have peeled right to go to his house.

"Where you going?" I yelled.

"Come on, I want to show you something."

I followed him past Aunt Goldie's, past Miss Stevens' and the McWhirters'. Across the street, Allison Haddad and her mother waved at us as they carried groceries in from the car.

"Big storm coming," Mrs. Haddad called out. "Better get home."

Allison looked away, embarrassed.

"What are we stopping here for?" I asked when Arthur braked at Mrs. Smiley's.

"Come on, you got to see something."

We went up the sidewalk and stepped quietly onto

the broad front porch of Belle Smiley's old house. Hers was the sort of place that, on Halloween, you halfway didn't want to trick-or-treat. It always looked so spooky under those giant cottonwood trees.

"Arthur, you nuts or something?" I said in a hoarse voice. "You're not going to ask her for cookies!" (We'd done that once or twice in our lives.)

"Don't you notice anything different?" Arthur asked, standing there with a dumb smile on his face.

I looked around, but I couldn't see much. It was dark as a skunk's insides on that porch.

Then Arthur was pushing the doorbell.

"I'll let Mrs. Smiley tell you," he said, and he pushed the bell a second time. "There's a light on. Looks like she's back in the kitchen."

"I'll bet she's turned off her hearing aid. Let's get out of here."

Then Arthur pointed to the new aluminum storm door with a screen on the top half.

"You've got to be more observant, Dan."

"What is this," I croaked, "an I.Q. test?"

"Yeah, and you just flunked."

I could sense Arthur's disappointment in me, so I stood there, observing Mrs. Smiley's door the way he wanted me to. *What am I doing here?* I kept thinking. All I'd wanted was to see Stacey Darlington in her natural habitat.

Mrs. Smiley must have heard us all right, because another light went on inside. We could see her crossing the living room, sort of swaying from side to side the way she does. She's just a little bitty thing, but with legs like parentheses, she walks funny.

"Who is it?" she called as she came along.

Arthur answered. "It's me, Mrs. Smiley. Me and Dan."

"Oh, my!" She opened the door. "Isn't this nice? Won't you come in?"

"We're on our way to my house, but Dan wanted to see your new door."

I did?

Mrs. Smiley flicked on the porch light so I could see. "Isn't it a beauty?" she asked.

Then she demonstrated the lock and explained how her new door didn't squeak, didn't slam, didn't swell up and get stuck in the kind of drippy, drizzly weather we'd been having.

"Wow!" I exclaimed, starting to be impressed.

I pictured Mrs. Smiley's original door. Inside a green wooden frame was this screen with fourteen patches on it by actual count—one of them dating back as far as World War II. She had sewed her patches on with different colors of yarn, which she said attracted the butterflies.

"I sure hated to part with my old door"—she sighed—"after the years of service it gave me, but when my son came visiting from Ohio, he insisted." She shook her head sadly. " 'Why don't you get rid of that old eyesore?' is the way *he* put it."

Finally there wasn't anything else to talk about, and the wind was threatening to blow her over. She made us promise to tell our mothers hello. I was supposed to remind mine that Mrs. Smiley would need her hair set Friday morning because of our Presbyterian church bazaar.

"I only have two days to finish my needlepoint cushion," she told us, "but it'll bring a fancy price when it's done."

We started edging off the porch.

"Come see me again," she said, and we told her we would.

"Know what she did with her old screen door?" Arthur asked as we got back on our bikes.

"What?"

"She gave it to me."

"She did? That old thing? What for?"

"It's a work of art, man!"

I ought to worry about him, I remember thinking.

At the Darlingtons' everything was as usual—chaotic. They weren't exactly the Brady Bunch, but they sure could have used a good maid like Alice.

We stepped over Gwyn and Theo, who had paper dolls spread all over the living-room floor.

"Don't walk on Prince Ragnor," Gwyn squealed, covering the royal wardrobe with her fat little body.

Tabby was practicing the piano, her fingers flying up and down the keyboard, doing scales.

Ronnie Vae was folded up in a big chair in the corner, having a giggly phone conversation with some other ten-year-old.

I looked around for Stacey, trying not to be obvious about it, but she was nowhere in sight. She pretty much lived with her friend Evelyn the way Arthur lived with me. And Mr. Darlington was only home on Sundays, so I didn't bother looking for him. He grows plants at the Lewis Greenscape during the day and is maintenance foreman at the National Guard Armory at night.

"It takes a lot of money," Arthur always says, "to keep food on our table."

And that's where we found Arthur's mother—at the kitchen table, pushing Angélique back and forth in the stroller, reading a book, and eating potato salad at the same time. I really like Mrs. Darlington.

She's one of those soft cushiony types with a round face and pink cheeks who's as nice to her kids' friends as she is to her kids.

Arthur headed for the fridge, so I sat down on a stool nearby.

"Is that a new book, Mrs. Darlington?" I asked politely. She always liked to tell me about her books, romances she bought ten at a time with her groceries.

"Oh, yes, Danny," she said, shaking her head, "and I'm so disgusted with it."

"How come?"

"I've read to page one fourteen and *still* nothing's happened. I mean, you know, by page one fourteen something ought to be happening." She took another forkful of salad. "Old Shirley Mulhollow really let me down this time!"

"Can I sleep over at Dan's tonight?" Arthur asked as he handed me a slice of bologna wrapped around a pickle.

"Only if you're invited," she answered.

Then she was off again, flipping to page 115, looking for something to happen.

And that's the way it was last summer, the third of June. Without knowing it, we were all waiting for something to happen. I guess that's life, huh? The whole world is waiting around to see what will happen next. But even Shirley Mulhollow—who had sold 250,000 copies of *Love's Searing Flames*, according to the book cover—couldn't have imagined what was about to take place in Grand Island, Nebraska.

Before Arthur and I got back to my house, televisions up and down the street were announcing tornado sightings in the vicinity, but some of us didn't hear that first weather report. Mom was busy sewing; Karen Darlington was glued to her paperback; Mrs. Smiley was no doubt hunkered over her needlepoint. My grandparents, we later learned, were both out in the shed watching Dad work on the tractor. Grandma was delivering a pot of coffee to them about that time. Nobody knew for sure where Aunt Goldie was that night . . . or the next. *Or* the next.

Eight O'clock

Arthur and I flipped on the TV as soon as we got back to my house. He chucked the sack containing his clean socks and Fruit-of-the-Loom underwear onto the sofa, then stretched out there himself.

"Channel five or ten-eleven?" I asked.

"Ten-eleven."

I moved his feet and sat down next to him.

I could hear Mom out in the kitchen, sewing away on Grandma Hatch's birthday dress. Click-clack.

Clickety-clack. Fast, then slow, then a long humming stretch where Mom gunned it for all she was worth. Arthur made one of his terrific accelerating noises, and we both doubled up.

The TV show had already started, but that rarely bothers Arthur and me. When we're watching something funny like *Laverne and Shirley* or *Happy Days*, we can tune in any old time.

When the first commercial came on, I went to the kitchen for some potato chips. I couldn't believe what I saw there. The curtains at the kitchen window were blowing straight in. They looked like something a cartoonist might draw.

"Hey!" I shouted for Mom to look. "Isn't that crazy?"

I leaned over the sink to peer out, but superbreeze nearly flattened me.

"Would you close that, please?" Mom said. "It's suffocate or blow away, one or the other. You put your bike in the garage, I hope."

"Yup."

I opened the cupboard where we kept the chips.

"You suppose Dad and Grandpa got the tractor running yet?" I asked.

"Probably."

She lifted the presser foot, and I heard her snip-ping threads. If Arthur hadn't been there, I'd have sat down and watched her sew. I loved her new machine. It was the last thing she bought before she quit at the hair boutique. She really knew how to operate it, too. Forward, reverse, flip, snip. Zig-zag, ziiiiig-zaaaaaaaaag, zg-zg, zg-zg-zg-zg.

I made zig-zagging motions in the air until Mom asked what in the world I was doing. Then I remembered why I had come into the kitchen in the first place.

"We're out of chips, Dan, if that's what you want."

I settled for soda crackers.

I watched Mom as she held the top half of the lavender dress at arm's length to inspect it.

"I wonder if Mother Hatch wants this skirt gathered or pleated," she said, more to herself.

"Why not do both?" I suggested.

Mom grinned. She blew a strand of hair out of her face, then pushed back her chair and went to the phone. "I'll be sorry if I don't ask her."

"That's funny," I heard her say a minute later.

I looked up from spreading peanut butter on crackers to see her staring at the mouthpiece. She clicked the little chrome piece up and down, then dialed again.

"Now it's ringing, but no one's answering," she

mumbled. "Where would Grandma Hatch be on a night like this?"

I shrugged and carried my plate of crackers back to the living room.

Arthur was so glad for the arrival of food that we almost missed the severe-weather announcement coming over the TV.

". . . in the St. Paul area, just north of Grand Island . . ." I heard that much.

Mom rushed in through the dining area. "Listen!" she shushed us.

". . . in effect until further notice is given. Warnings are being issued for St. Paul, Dannebrog, and surrounding rural areas. Funnel clouds have been sighted near Dannebrog. Persons in those vicinities are urged to take all possible precautions."

Mom had her hand over her heart. "St. Paul's northwest, thank God!"

Arthur sat up, his eyes round.

"Grandpa's farm is east, close to Phillips," I explained.

"St. Paul's still too close for comfort," Mom added.

"Do we have to go to the basement?" I asked. Now that we were all set for the next show, I hoped not.

Mom didn't answer. She had her face right up against our big front window, shielding her eyes, trying to see out. Normally she's a lot more casual about storms than Dad is, but she looked worried.

"It's pitch-black out there," she said. "I've never seen it so dark this early."

It was noisy outside as well as dark. Our shake shingles, flapping and smacking overhead, made me think somebody was up there playing a xylophone on the roof. Minerva didn't like the weather, either. She was crouched under Dad's chair with her ears back. No wonder. She'd be carried off like a tumbleweed in one of our stiff prairie winds. I was glad when Mom pulled the drapes for us.

"Do we *have* to go downstairs?" I asked again.

"Not yet, Danny. We'll keep listening to the TV."

Arthur spoke up: "Tornadoes move from southwest to northeast, remember?"

I remembered. Our science class had taken a field trip in April to visit the weather service out at the airport. The meteorologist had shown us how they get the hook echo on radar, how they post a watch, all that technical stuff.

Arthur made arm motions toward a plant hanging in the corner of the room. "It'll head off that way someplace."

His expert opinion should have made me feel better, but it didn't.

He helped himself to another cracker, then settled back into the sofa cushions. *He* wasn't worried.

Mom's forehead puckered as she walked away. I knew what was on her mind. We were both wishing Dad was home.

We watched TV another few minutes, but I couldn't get into it like before. Not that I was scared, exactly. I'd been through dozens of tornado watches in my life and nothing ever happened, though a barn roof got rearranged over in Clay Center one year. Every spring, practically, we have to "hit for the cellar," as Grandpa puts it. But when a tornado watch changes to a warning, and when the siren starts . . . well . . . that's when things aren't so mellow anymore.

"Shouldn't you call your mother, Arthur?" Mom said to him after trying the phone again. "I'm not sure she'd want you to stay here tonight."

"Oh, Mom!" I groaned. (There I was, thinking the sun rose and set on me.)

"Wait, I'd better call Goldie first," she said. "Someone should run over and check on Mrs. Smiley. When she turns that hearing aid down . . ."

After a while she hung up again. "Doesn't anybody stay home?" she muttered.

By then I was standing in the kitchen doorway, trying to tell her Aunt Goldie had probably gone bowling.

"Who you calling now?" I asked instead. Her attacks on the phone were suddenly more interesting than what was happening in living color on the nineteen-inch screen.

"Mrs. Smiley. Ssssh . . ."

"She's trying to finish a needlepoint cushion for the Presbyterians," Arthur piped up from the sofa.

"Yeah," I whispered in Mom's face, remembering, "and I'm supposed to tell you not to forget she's coming Friday for you to fix her hair."

All the while Mom was waving her hand for us to be quiet, so I backed away.

Next thing I knew she was at the hall closet, putting her red Windbreaker on over her jeans and Hastings College T-shirt.

"She doesn't answer," she said. "I'm driving over there to make sure she has her TV on. I won't be long. Now listen, both of you."

We listened. She was using a very firm voice.

"I want you to take this flashlight"—she got it off the shelf and handed it to me—"and a blanket and put them in the downstairs bathroom. I want you

44

to do it *this minute!*" I nodded, trying the flashlight to make sure it worked.

"If the siren starts, get Ryan and go downstairs. Don't wake him up if you can help it, all right?"

Arthur's eyes got big listening to Mom. He told me once they never go to the basement during windstorms. That figures. They moved here from California, what do they know? Ever hear of a tornado in good old CA?

Mom went to get a blanket.

"I'll be right back," she told us, hooking her purse on her shoulder. "I'm sure nothing's going to happen, but we have to be prepared, right? Your father would have a fit if we ignored the siren."

She smiled and waved her car keys at us as she left, barely squeezing out before the door slammed shut again.

"Whooeeeee!" Arthur exclaimed. "Sounds like my bull-roarer outside!"

I hurried downstairs with the emergency stuff and set it on the bathroom counter. Minerva went with me, scurrying across my feet on the steps, acting the way she does when she wants attention.

I picked her up by the middle, smoothed down her stripes, and balanced her on the glass door of the shower. Usually she'll do a tightrope act for me, but she only yowled and jumped off. After giving me her mean jungle look, she sat down to dig at her ear.

"You got a flea in there?" I asked, bending to give her a good scratching.

She didn't like that, either.

Upstairs, Arthur was hooting and hollering again. I decided I was missing all the good parts, so I hurried up the two short flights of steps, with Minerva dashing ahead of me.

Sometime in there, in the middle of all that comedy on the screen, the siren began. Now, *that* is a very sobering sound. It's unlike anything else, having its own built-in chill factor.

I thought of Mom first. She'd hear it and come back, I told myself.

Then I thought of Dad and how far the farm was from town. They wouldn't even hear the siren out there.

In half a second, I was at the phone, dialing 555-2379.

Four rings. Then I heard Grandma's voice.

"Grandma!" I shouted into the phone. "Where have you been? There's a tornado just north of G.I. The siren's going, can you hear it?"

A voice said something, but it sounded so far away.

"Talk louder, Grandma! I can't hear you."

The voice faded away entirely. I wasn't even sure it was Grandma's now.

"There's a tornado coming! Can you hear me?"

Finally, there wasn't anything on the line but the sound of another phone ringing very faintly, as if it were in New York or someplace far away. I couldn't figure it out.

By then, Arthur was standing next to me. I was just about to hand him the phone when, abruptly, the siren stopped. It didn't taper off, it just quit, as if someone snipped it with scissors. Except for the TV, everything around us suddenly seemed very still.

"Hey," he said, raising his eyebrows, "they changed their minds."

I hung up the phone. I didn't know what was happening.

"Maybe they got their weather signals crossed," he suggested happily. "They could, you know. I read a book once about that happening, where this whole fleet of fishing boats put out to sea . . ." he rattled on.

I ran to the door, thinking I might see Mom pulling into the driveway, but no luck.

"It's quit blowing," I called over my shoulder to Arthur.

Sure enough, the wind had died down. Maybe the storm wouldn't amount to anything after all.

That nice comforting thought had hardly entered my mind when the siren blared forth again. With a jolt, I remembered what Mom had told us to do.

"We always turn on the radio," Arthur said, already on his way to the kitchen. "You want me to? I'll get the weather station."

I was hardly listening. I hurried down the bedroom hallway to Ryan's room at the end. I hated like everything to get him up. He'd cry. I knew he'd wake up and cry. Without Mom, Arthur and I would have him screaming in our ears the whole time.

When I saw him in his crib, peacefully sleeping on the side of his face, his rear end in the air, I just didn't have the heart to wake him up. I'd wait a minute or two. Mom would be back. Anyway, it's blowing over, I told myself, it won't last.

Quietly, I closed the door behind me.

That's when the lights started flickering.

In the hallway, I practically had a head-on with Arthur, who was coming at me real fast. The look on his face scared me.

"There's no . . . there's no . . ."

"What?"

"There's no radio reception anymore. It just went dead! This guy . . . He kept saying, 'Tornado alert, tornado alert!' Then it went dead."

We rushed back to the living room. The TV was flashing these big letters that filled the entire screen: CD . . . CD . . . CD . . .

"What's it mean?" Arthur cried.

"Civil Defense Emergency!" I whirled around. "I'm getting Ryan!"

The lights flickered again.

At the same time we heard these really strange sounds that stopped us in our tracks. They were coming from the bathroom and the kitchen. Sucking sounds. The drains were sucking! I felt this awful pulling in my ears, too, as if there were vacuums on both sides of my head.

"I've got to go home!" Arthur cried all of a sudden, bolting for the door.

I ran after him. "You're not—you can't!" I grabbed the back of his T-shirt, hauled him around, and pushed him toward the stairs. "Get *down* there. I have to get Ryan! Now *go!*"

I don't know what I'd have done if he hadn't minded me. We were catching the fear from each other, and even though the siren was screaming on and off again, so I didn't know what it was telling us, I knew we had to take cover fast.

The lights went out for good just before I reached Ryan's room.

Nine O'clock

I smashed face first into Ryan's butterfly mobile. That's how I knew I was at the crib. I felt for him, got my hands under his nightshirt and diaper, rolled him over. I lifted him, but we didn't get far. He was caught in the mobile, his arm or his head . . . I couldn't see . . . I couldn't get him loose. . . .

"Mom!" I yelled, though I knew she wasn't there.

I tried to lay him down again, but he was so tangled, part of him was still up in the air. He started to cry.

"Wait, Ryan, I'll get you out!" But I couldn't.

Finally, holding him with my left arm, I climbed onto the side of the crib. My right hand followed the string up the mobile, way up to the hook. I yanked it loose. The whole thing came crashing down on top of us as I jumped backward off the crib.

The plastic butterfly poking me was poking Ryan, too, but I didn't care. The tornado was close, and I knew it. Both my ears had popped, and I had this crazy fear that those drains, sucking like monsters now, would get us if the storm didn't.

Arthur was at the bottom of the stairs, waiting. Thank God he'd found the flashlight! I jumped the last half-flight to the floor.

"Hurry!" I screamed. I swung into the doorway of the bathroom, with Arthur right behind me. We crouched under the towel rack.

"Shine it here, on Ryan," I gasped. "He's caught in this thing." By now Ryan was kicking and screaming, and his eyes were big in the light.

Once we got the mess of strings free of Ryan's sweaty nightshirt, Arthur kicked the mobile against the wall by the toilet.

"I have to go home!" he cried. "They won't go to the basement. Mama never does."

The beam of light bounced around the blackness of the bathroom as Arthur scrambled to his feet, but I grabbed and held on to him.

"You can't go! It's here! Can't you feel it?"

The siren quit again as I pulled him back down and threw my leg over him. The flashlight clattered to the floor and rolled away from us.

We heard it next. The lull. The deadliest quiet ever, one that makes you think you might explode. The heat in that room built until I couldn't get my breath.

Then I began to hear noises. A chair scraping across the kitchen floor upstairs.

"Your mom's back!" Arthur said, pushing at my leg.

I knew it wasn't my mother moving the chair.

The noises got worse. It seemed as if every piece of furniture was moving around up there . . . big, heavy things, smashing into each other.

A window popped.

Crash! Another.

Glass, shattering—everywhere—right next to us in the laundry room.

I pulled a towel down over Ryan and held him tight. If he was still crying, I didn't know it because

I was *feeling* the sucking this time. It was like something trying to lift my body right up off the floor.

Arthur felt it, too. "Mother of God!" He crossed himself. "We're going to die!"

Ten seconds more and that howling, shrieking tornado was upon us.

"The blanket!" I screamed at Arthur's ear.

He pulled it down from the countertop and we covered ourselves, our hands shaking wildly. I wasn't worrying about my mom then or my dad or Mrs. Smiley. Just us. Ryan and Arthur and me, huddled together there on the floor.

The roaring had started somewhere to the east, then came bearing down on us like a hundred freight trains. Only that twister didn't move on. It stationed itself right overhead, making the loudest noise I'd ever heard, whining worse than any jet. There was a tremendous crack, and I felt the wall shudder behind us. I knew then our house was being ripped apart. Suddenly chunks of ceiling were falling on our heads.

We'll be buried! was all I could think.

At that moment, as plain as anything above that deafening roar, I heard my dad's voice: *The shower's the safest place.*

I didn't question hearing it. Holding Ryan against

me with one arm, I began crawling toward the shower stall. I reached back and yanked at Arthur's shirt. Somehow we got inside with the blanket. Another explosion, and the glass shower door shattered all over the bathroom floor.

We pulled the blanket over our heads and I began to pray. Out loud, though I couldn't hear my own voice: "God help us, God help us." I said it over and over, into Ryan's damp hair, my lips moving against his head. I knew Arthur was praying, too, jammed there into my side. I could feel Ryan's heart beating through his undershirt against mine. *My* heart was thanking God for making me go back for him, but not in words. Outside those places where our bodies touched, there was nothing but terror as the roar of that tornado went on and on. I thought the world was coming to an end, *had* come to an end, and so would we, any minute.

Then I felt Ryan's fat fingers close around one of mine. He pulled my hand to his mouth and started sucking on my finger. It made me cry. The tears ran down my cheeks and onto his head. With the whole world blowing to pieces around us, Ryan took my hand and made me feel better.

Afterward, neither Arthur nor I was able to say how long we huddled there in the basement shower.

"A tornado's forward speed is generally thirty to fifty miles an hour," the meteorologist had told us.

Our tornado's forward speed was zero. It parked right there on Sand Crane Drive. Five minutes or ten, we couldn't tell, but it seemed like an hour. Roaring and humming and shrieking, that twister was right on top of us. I'll never be that scared again as long as I live. Neither will Arthur.

When at last the noise began to let up, Arthur jerked out from under the blanket, leaned across me to the opening of the shower, and vomited into the broken glass and Sheetrock. The glow from the half-buried flashlight showed his head bobbing again and again.

Squeamish as I am about something like that, I wasn't revolted. I wondered if I had wet my pants myself. I couldn't tell for sure because water had started rising under us in the shower. My shoes and jeans were both soaked. I had to move Ryan, who was wriggling to be put down, way up on my shoulder.

"Arthur," I said, my voice shaking, but thinking to encourage him, "we made it . . . we're alive!"

I looked away as he heaved again.

Arthur was still doubled over the Sheetrock

mess when the hail began. Once it got going, it hit us with the force of buckshot. That fast I knew the kitchen upstairs was gone, floor and all. Those marble-size hailstones were pouring in from somewhere. I thought of Mom's new sewing machine . . . and my bike.

It didn't take long for Arthur to crawl back beside me, but even under the blanket those hailstones hurt like crazy, smacking our heads and shoulders. We huddled together to protect Ryan, who was down in my lap again.

Suddenly I was hit with a sickness worse than Arthur's. Mom! Where was she? Did she get to Smiley's?

"Arthur!" I cried, sitting up straight. "My mom!"

"My . . . whole family," he choked out.

In that second I could see my mother's car hurtling through the air, see it ripping open, the black funnel sucking her out and swirling her away. I could hear her *scream!*

I started crying. "She can't be dead, she can't be!" I hit my head against the tile to make the pictures stop.

"Shut up!" Arthur shouted. "Just shut up, will you?"

He pulled away so we weren't touching and drew himself into the opposite corner of the shower. I didn't care. I felt as if someone had reached down my throat and turned me inside out.

Another terrifying thought slammed into my head: What if we were the only ones alive? Three of us, out of 38,000 people—an entire city gone, bodies strewn all the way to the river. . . .

Chills raced up my arms. I was shaking all over.

At least—I scrabbled for something to hang on to—*at least I still have my dad!* He'd be safe, wouldn't he, out on the farm?

With a rush I thought of everyone else. Stacey . . . and Angélique, not even a year old . . . and all the Darlingtons in between.

"Jesus, Mary, and Joseph, have mercy on us."

I heard Arthur's prayer above the ripping and rattling of the storm and knew he wasn't thinking of himself.

I clenched my teeth to keep from going to pieces. Please, God, please, I begged, make everyone okay!

Overhead, the storm continued to rage. The sharp sound of hail striking tile went on and on, and I began to wonder if we might just be battered to death. Now and then, a finger of wind reached into our hiding place, flipping the blanket until we'd anchored it under us again. I shuddered and pulled up my knees, shifting the baby once more. With the temperature dropping and the water rising, we couldn't stay in the shower stall forever. What were we going to do?

Only Ryan had recovered enough to be himself and was dabbling one hand in the water, making happy noises. Once I got him into a standing position against my knees, he began "talking" and stretching under the blanket tent. *He* wasn't worried. I wiped my tears on the back of his undershirt. What does he know? I thought, for a second wishing I could trade places with him. He wouldn't even remember this night.

As Ryan bunched up in my lap to jump, I took hold of his hands to steady him. I made little balls of his fists and felt how small they were inside my big twelve-year-old hands. Suddenly it occurred to me that I had saved his life. I *had!* I warmed myself on that thought as I rubbed my cheek against his head. He was so little. As he bounced and gurgled, I could see why Mom liked him so much.

That was when I remembered Minerva. My cat! Oh, no! Had she followed us downstairs? But a cat would find a place—wouldn't she?—to ride out the storm. Cats are smart. They can take care of themselves. She's all right! I convinced myself, because I couldn't bear to think otherwise.

The hard peppering sounds of the hail were growing slushier, softer. The hail was turning to rain. Quickly I slipped the blanket off my head. My gosh, there was the night sky where the bathroom ceiling had been! I shivered as icy raindrops splatted in my face and went streaking down my neck. Somehow, *seeing* was worse than *knowing*.

"Arthur—" I nudged him with my foot—"look up there!"

He pulled the blanket off and tipped back his head.

We sat there, blinking into the rain as the blanket bobbed up and down over Ryan.

The Next Hour or So

We were soaking wet and getting colder by the minute. Already water had risen two or three inches in the shower. I knew we couldn't stay there much longer. Ryan needed dry clothes. I had to find Mom.

"Listen," Arthur said, now that things had quieted a little, "do you hear water running?"

I'd been hearing it: water gurgling and splashing onto the cement floor.

"Pipes are broken," he said.

"Let's go," I said through chattering teeth, though I didn't have any idea where.

Arthur got out ahead of me, carefully picking his way across the bathroom rubble. He held up something shiny—our towel rack, bent like a boomerang. With that he dug among chunks of Sheetrock for the flashlight, which miraculously was still on.

"Want me to check around first?" he asked.

"No, wait, I'm coming." I got stiffly to my feet and shifted Ryan so that he wouldn't brush against the jagged edge of the shower door. "If the stairs are clear, we can walk right on up, like always." Ryan patted my face. He was as glad to be up and moving as I was.

The first shock was Arthur's, because he had the flashlight. When I pushed into the doorway beside him, I caught my breath. Our house was gone. Roof, walls, floor—gone! As far as I could see, only the cement foundation remained. Inside the foundation—surrounding us and blocking our way—was a jungle of fallen support beams and splintered wood. I figured the rec room and the big storage area were just as bad.

"Pickup sticks," Arthur said quietly.

I couldn't speak. I just stood there, letting the horrible truth soak in.

Our furniture, clothes, books were haphazardly mixed into the wreckage. Papers were scattered everywhere. Like white bats, they fluttered up and over the foundation in the gusting wind. A tangle of two-by-fours barricaded us in the bathroom.

Arthur stepped over a paint can and kicked aside a striped towel I'd never seen before. In a half-strangled voice he said, "You can't bring Ryan out here."

"I can't leave him in the bathroom by himself!" I couldn't stay behind, didn't Arthur know that? I was scared. I had to get out to find my mom.

He didn't argue when I followed him. Besides, he needed my help to open up even the skinniest passage alongside the bathroom wall. With Ryan on my left arm, my right one was free to help Arthur twist aside the boards. The loose stuff we threw over the partition in the direction of a storage area.

We hadn't cleared three feet toward the stairs before we knew we'd gone as far as we could in that direction. Dad's rocker-lounger was wedged into the basement hallway ahead of us, buried under a ton of stuff. Somebody's camper shell rested on top of it all.

"I can't budge it," Arthur groaned after several tries at moving the camper top.

I slumped against the wall, totally discouraged. "The stairs are buried, too," I said. "They'd have to be."

Arthur climbed up onto the arm of Dad's chair. He covered the west foundation from one end to the other with the light. "Gosh, Dan, look at that!"

Outlined against the black sky, the northwest corner walls of our house, the only ones still attached, sagged freakishly toward each other. I thought of skin flaps curling over a wound. It made me sick to look at it.

"Ryan's room," I said, "the bunny wallpaper."

As much as I wanted my mom and dad right then, I was glad they weren't there to see all I was seeing. They loved our house as much as I did.

Ryan shivered and drew up his knees.

Suddenly I had an idea. "Arthur, could we climb out over that pile of bricks on the other side?"

He shone the light onto the avalanche of buff-colored bricks along the west wall. "How do we get there?"

Just then a low, moaning sound raised hackles on the back of my neck. Arthur jumped off the chair. We froze. The noise rumbled to a crescendo right over our heads, making us jump when it crashed. Thunder! My lord, it was only thunder!

"Take Ryan a minute," I said, recovering enough to trade him for the flashlight. "I'll be right back."

I left them at the bathroom door and snaked my way alongside the hallway heading north, ducking and burrowing under debris when I had to. If I could just get to that brick pile . . .

Glass crunched underfoot with every step, and I kept getting snagged by things I couldn't see. Once I fell and dropped the flashlight in the water. I scraped myself good trying to get it again.

The biggest hurdle was a mass of wet carpeting—gold shag from our living room. Or the upstairs hall. I pushed against it. It was too soggy, too heavy. I'd have to crawl over.

"Ow, ouch!" I cried as something gouged me in the leg.

"You okay?" Arthur yelled.

"I'm okay," I answered back, glad he couldn't see my face.

My jeans were ripped, and I was bleeding, but the wound wasn't mortal, as Arthur would say. I kicked viciously at the board with the ugly nails sticking out. How in the world would we get Ryan out without hurting him? The basement was a stupid obstacle course—a death trap!

I stood there a minute, breathing hard, wondering

what to do next. It was raining again, and I was shaking—from the cold, from being so scared. The tops of my hands stung with scrapes, and blood trickled down my leg. Were we trapped? Of course, there was always the bathroom. Standing on the toilet on the outside wall, we could probably help each other out. But what about Ryan? Could we hoist him up or something?

In the lightning that tore across the sky every few minutes, I could see the clouds were still low and boiling. I didn't know if we'd be safe anywhere, even when we got out. I wanted my mom and dad so much!

And I wanted Minerva. . . .

I swung the light around, probing the dark recesses for two bright eyes. I shot the beam higher up, remembering how she hated water.

"Here, kitty," I whispered.

I tried using my high kitty-calling voice, but my throat closed off. In my heart, I knew it was no use. She was gone. No way could a lightweight like Minerva survive a tornado.

I slid down on my heels, pushing my face into the wet carpet. *I don't know what to do.* Hot tears squeezed out of my eyes. What in the world was I supposed to do?

From somewhere came the wail of sirens dipping in and out on the wind. At first the sound made me feel worse than ever. Death . . . fire . . . God help us.

Then my head jerked up. *Sirens!* That meant people were alive out there. Someone was coming to help! Were they police cars? Ambulances? *I can't give up now!*

"Dan, what are you doing?" Arthur called, and I remembered I'd left him in the dark. "I think I can smell gas."

I straightened, sniffed. My nose was too clogged up. I couldn't smell anything. I sniffed again. With gas escaping we could have an explosion! We could be gassed just by breathing.

Whirling around, I snagged my other leg, but I didn't stop, I just went crashing back to where Arthur and Ryan were waiting.

"We can't get through," I said with fresh panic. "Can you smell gas?"

"I can't tell, but there'll be gas leaking out if water is, right?"

Ryan was stiffening and throwing his head back, going "unnnnhhh." The crying would start any second.

"He's blue," Arthur said, jouncing him up and

down. "Can't we find something dry to wrap him in?"

That, on top of everything else.

My mind was threshing so bad I couldn't think straight.

"Waaaahhh!" Ryan cried.

All of a sudden I remembered the stack of towels Mom kept under the sink. I could wrap him in one of those. I pushed past Arthur, knelt, wrenched the cupboard open enough to reach one hand in, and pulled out a towel.

"It's dry!" I yelled, thrilled to have something go right.

We couldn't lay Ryan down on the countertop, which was covered with broken mirror, so Arthur sat on the toilet seat and held him. I left his undershirt on, but worked his wet diaper off over his hips. Then, with Arthur's help, I got the towel wrapped around him twice.

I held him close, rocking and shushing him the way I'd seen Mom do it. He snuggled into my chest. He didn't know it, but he was warming me as much as I was warming him.

In the meantime, Arthur was doing the thinking for all of us. "Hey, I've got an idea," he said.

I never got to hear what it was. Just then a light

appeared overhead, bobbing up and down with someone's steps.

Coming closer, the light swept over our heads, across the west foundation, onto the sagging walls.

"HELP!" Arthur yelled at once, too close to Ryan's ear.

The baby screamed.

"We're down here!" he yelled again.

"*Arthur!* Dear God, is that you?"

Hope shot through me like an electric charge. Arthur was jumping up and down. *"Mama?"*

"It's me, Stacey!"

Arthur shot the light straight up in the sky, waving it around like a beacon.

Seconds later, Stacey was looking down on us from above, and we were lighting up each other's faces, which didn't need lighting up at all. We would have glowed in the dark, we were so glad to see each other.

"Where's Mama? Is she okay? What about—"

"Everyone's okay, now that I've found *you!*"

For the first time, Arthur burst into tears. Big sobs racked his body. He couldn't have held them back if he'd tried.

"We were so worried," Stacey said, half sobbing herself. "We tried to get you on the phone, before—"

"I thought you were all . . . *dead*!" Arthur gulped. "I didn't think you'd go downstairs."

"Oh, Arthur, we didn't! There wasn't time. Mama tried to get everyone under the big bed, but she and Ronnie and I wouldn't fit. We had to flatten out on the floor—it was awful! We were lying there, holding each other, Arthur—" Her voice broke. "Ronnie Vae got sucked right out the window."

I gasped.

"I tried to hang on to her, but I couldn't. I couldn't do anything but scream."

"Stacey! Is she all right?"

"She is! It's a pure miracle! It threw her into the Winegars' bushes, knocked her right out." Stacey wiped her face, her hand shaking so hard we could see it from below. "Mama thinks she doesn't even remember it."

I shuddered. I could feel that sucking tornado all over again, I could *see* Ronnie. . . .

Ryan let out a first-class wail about then that sent all of us into action. Stacey leaned over the foundation and spotted the toilet tank with her big flashlight.

"Listen, Dan," she said, gulping hard, "can you climb up on that john with Ryan?"

I nodded.

In a second she was straddling the foundation, the torch positioned on the cement in front of her. The wind tossed rain in our faces and sent her black hair flying as I scrambled onto the toilet seat.

"Hand the baby up to me first," she said, "then I'll help you guys."

I climbed onto the narrow toilet tank. Bracing myself against the wall, with Stacey holding on to the neck of my T-shirt, I managed to take Ryan when Arthur lifted him up to me. I had to grab hold of Stacey's leg once to keep from toppling over, but we got the job done.

Right away she rewrapped him. "Poor little guy," she crooned, "he's practically naked, isn't he?"

A few minutes later, Arthur and I were climbing over all this stuff in the laundry room, with Stacey directing us. The window there had blown out clean as a whistle, frame and all, and the washing machine gave us something to stand on. In no time we were at ground level, shining our lights over the unbelievable rubble.

Our yard looked like a World War II battlefield. Next to the flattened garage, Dad's prized white Corvette lay on its top like a discarded matchbox toy. Somewhere under that trash heap, I knew, was my bike. My beloved ten-speed racer.

When I saw our big maple tree—uprooted and stripped clean—lying on the ground, I really hit rock bottom. Hooked on one branch was a scrap of lavender cloth. I guess seeing that top half of Grandma's birthday dress snapping and twisting in the wind made me sadder than anything. It was like . . . well . . . like seeing unfinished dreams, I guess.

"The whole neighborhood's gone," Stacey said, flashing onto the scrambled walls of the house next door, then onto a section of roof lying across our driveway. Wreckage was scattered in every direction as far as we could see.

Stacey handed me the torch so she could snap her dad's big denim jacket around Ryan.

"Stacey, I have to find my mom," I blurted out suddenly.

"What do you mean? Don't you *know* where she is? I thought you were home alone, tending Ryan."

I could feel the corners of my mouth pulling down. I turned away, so Arthur had to tell her for me. When he finished, he asked Stacey if she could take Ryan to their house so the two of us could go look for Mom.

"Arthur!" she exclaimed. "We don't have a house anymore!"

His jaw dropped. "We don't?"

"All that's left is a few walls. The whole neighborhood looks like this."

It was Arthur's turn to be speechless. I know how sick it sounds, but somehow, hearing such bad news made me feel better. We were all in the same boat. We were *all* homeless.

Slowly, we began picking our way toward the street.

"Where's Mama now?" Arthur asked.

"Patrol cars were down at the end of the block right after the tornado, loading people up. We took the kids down there. I begged her to let me come to Dan's and look for you. She said if I found you, we should get out fast, any way we could. It's too dangerous to stay here."

I stopped right in front of her. "I'm not leaving without my mom!"

"Of course not, Dan. We'll find her, you'll see." By then Stacey had her arm around me, giving me a squeeze that made me want to cry all over again. "I'll bet she's waiting out the storm at Smiley's right now."

A blast of wind plastered my wet clothes to my body, triggering a bad case of the shakes. I prayed to God she was right.

Once we got to the street, we took off running.

Or trying to run. Arthur and I were in front, Stacey right behind, with Ryan in his Levi's pouch. There was no time to think about what we might find between our house and Smiley's. We just took off.

Covering those three blocks was like reliving my worst nightmare. It must have taken us twenty minutes to get to the corner of Sand Crane Drive and Fonda Way, a distance I've clocked at one minute three seconds on my bike, two minutes four seconds running.

Remember those dreams where you're frantically trying to get away from someone and you can't move? In mine, it's always these great hulking linebackers in black jumpsuits who all tackle me at once. They won't let go of my legs, so I have to keep dragging them along. I'm yelling and screaming the whole time, but nobody ever comes to save me. Finally I wake up in a sweat just as they're ready to bash my brains out.

That night—rain-soaked, shaken by thunder that rolled across the sky like kettledrums—I kept telling myself this was only another nightmare. Pretty soon I'd wake up and laugh because none of it was true. But I knew I was feeding myself a lie. The truth was just too terrible, that's all. Everything on Sand Crane Drive was destroyed, and getting to Smiley's place fast was exactly like trying to escape in a bad dream.

All structures—houses, garages, fences, telephone poles—had been leveled, the debris scattered helter-skelter. The only buildings still standing were a line of apartments several blocks away that we could see when lightning flashed.

The trees on Sand Crane Drive were straight out of a nightmare, too. They looked as if some giant with a big, meaty hand had stripped the main branches and snapped off the rest. A few of the big trees had toppled clean over. Their shaggy root systems silhouetted against that electric sky looked like a landscape from a monster movie.

There was no sign of Mom anywhere. *Or* her silver Chevy Citation. Cars and trucks had been tossed about like toys up and down Sand Crane, but hers wasn't one of them.

We went a long time without stopping—stumbling, ducking things that were blowing loose. I fell a couple of times. We were so intent on sweeping both sides of the street with our lights, we sometimes crashed into each other in the dark.

"Mom . . . *Mom!*" I tried yelling at first, but the wind shredded my words. She'd never hear me over that howling, spitting storm.

Once my heart leaped. I thought I saw her. A figure caught on my light—someone thin, wearing jeans, hanging on to the back door of a van. When a man and a boy appeared and I recognized Jason Miller from school, I knew the lady wasn't my mom, but his.

They shone their light at us, and Jason's dad yelled, "Who is it?"

We slowed, answered back.

"Have you seen my mom?" I shouted.

They looked at each other, shook their heads.

Closer now, we could see they were inspecting their "Miller's Plumbing" van that had been slammed against a tree in their side yard.

Jason, shirttails flapping, appeared stunned at the sight of us running by.

Until Stacey got hit in the face with what she thought was a flying shingle, we hardly stopped at all. Then we had to. We made her sit down on the curb so Arthur could inspect the welt rising on her cheek, but Stacey only pushed him away. "I'm okay, you guys, really," she insisted, though she was blinking hard. I knew she was hurting.

"I can take Ryan," I offered as I gulped in the air. "Want me to?"

"No, he's fine." Stacey hooked her hair behind

her ears, sniffling a little, then awkwardly got to her feet. She hitched the baby up in place again.

"Look, Dan"—she pulled me over—"just look at him." I shone the light so I could see Ryan peeking out from inside her dad's jacket. He looked up at me so bright-eyed and solemn I had to smile.

"Isn't he something?" Stacey said with a grin. "I think he likes the ride."

And then we were off again.

When Arthur yelled a little later, "A person could get lost!" I knew what he meant. Without familiar landmarks, we'd long since lost track of who lived where.

At last we reached the corner of Fonda Way and Sand Crane, only to find the intersection there strewn with the litter of Aunt Goldie's house. All she had left was the bottom half of her yellow split-level. Not even that. Part of the lower level had been sheared off, too. Maybe Goldie had lucked out, not being home when it happened. I had to remind myself that none of us had lucked out. Not that night.

My heart was pounding hard as I leaped over the splintered wood covering Goldie's front yard. I had stopped being careful by then and was yelling for Mom once more. I couldn't get that picture out of my mind—her flying through the air. She could be buried anywhere. How would we know?

Arthur trailed me, both of us leaving Stacey behind.

Then I saw Mom's car and my heart quit beating altogether.

It was next door to Goldie's, in Miss Stevens' yard, a battered wreck wrapped in a length of chain-link fence.

"*Mom!*" I screamed, clambering over everything to get to it.

My hands shook wildly as I shone the light inside, over the backseat, across the floor. It was empty. Her purse lay on the front seat, covered with broken glass.

"Mom . . . Mom!" I cried, but the wind whipped the words out of my mouth.

Frantically, I started hauling stuff out from under the car. Boards and bricks and chunks of siding, throwing them anywhere, digging and crying until I couldn't see. I had to find her! She could be trapped . . . dying.

Arthur grabbed my arm from behind. "Come on, Dan," he yelled. "She made it to Smiley's, I know she did!"

I shook him off. I had to find her.

Then the two of them got hold of me and pulled

me away from the car. I kicked at Stacey, swore at Arthur, but they wouldn't let go.

Arthur wrestled the light out of my hand, dragged me along beside him. I knew she was there, buried under that car, I *knew* it. I didn't want to go on to Smiley's and waste all that time, but they wouldn't let go.

I was so crazy right then I didn't see the person in the red Windbreaker who was hurrying toward us.

"Look!" Stacey and Arthur shouted together.

My mom's voice screaming *"Danny!"*

Seconds later, I was in my mother's arms crying like a baby. Arthur and Stacey were crying, too, but Mom and I were the ones making most of the noise. You can't imagine how I felt right then.

We all had our arms around each other next. Mom was kissing everybody, including Ryan right through the denim jacket.

I figured then that nothing else mattered. You can do without all kinds of things—your house, your bike, your room, a whole city of people—if you have the ones you love.

Stacey, Arthur, and I got in each other's way trying to explain what it was like at our place and the Darlingtons'—all over Grand Island, for all we knew.

We snuffled and wiped our faces on our sleeves—even Mom—then smiled through our tears and hugged some more. It was really something!

Suddenly Mom noticed how wet I was and tried to get me to put on her Windbreaker, but I wouldn't. I told her I was used to it, which wasn't anywhere near the truth.

Right away then she had to have Ryan, so Stacey gave him up, and Mom started crying again once she had him in her arms, saying how thankful she was that we were all alive.

"What about Smiley?" Arthur asked.

"Oh, poor Smiley!" Mom said in a rush. "She's trapped downstairs in that house. I don't know how we're going to get her out."

We huddled there as she told us about it, rain running down our faces and into our mouths, all of us shaking.

She'd taken Mrs. Smiley to the basement and was on her way back to the car—which she'd parked at Goldie's, having looked for her sister first—when she actually saw the tornado coming. She ran back to Smiley's, the funnel practically at her heels. She told us how she'd dived under the dining-room table and held on to the legs as the storm raged on and on.

"I knew when the roof ripped off"—I felt Mom shudder—"but I didn't know until later that the back porch was gone, too, collapsed onto the stairs. When it was over, I called and called, but I couldn't get Belle to answer." I thought she was going to cry again. "I'm so worried about her. She could have had a heart attack down there and who'd know? It was pitch-black, and I couldn't get to her. . . . So I started for home. But without a light, I had to go back."

I began jumping around to warm up. My biggest worry right then was hypothermia. I was shaking so hard I couldn't stop.

"How can we leave Smiley?" Arthur began. "Maybe with flashlights . . ."

Stacey had gone out to the curb and was motioning and pointing.

"Mrs. Hatch, couldn't we get some help down there? That's where we took the kids right after."

Once in the street again, we could see lights and figures moving around a block or so beyond the Darlingtons' place. There was a bus, yellow lights flashing, and what looked like a fire truck. Other headlights lit up the intersection.

"Oh, thank God!" Mom said. "Danny, I died a thousand deaths . . ."

She didn't need to tell me. We put our arms around each other again. To think I'd almost left Ryan asleep in his room! I'd never tell her that. I reached across Mom and patted the warm round hump under the towel.

"Ryan Oliver." Saying his name almost choked me. I'd make sure he had the best big brother who ever lived, that's what I'd do.

By the time we got to the pickup corner, past the sad hulk of the Darlingtons' house, an ambulance and a patrol car had arrived. The school bus was waiting to take people to Kmart, we were told. An emergency center had been set up there. With sirens going and red lights pulsing, the area reminded me of a disaster scene on TV for sure.

The figures darting back and forth in the headlights turned out to be policemen, firemen, and Arthur's neighbors. A man got on the bullhorn, asking people to come out of their basements. Search and rescue was beginning, he said. He ticked off the dangers of staying, and there were plenty.

When he was finished, Mom and Stacey tried to tell him about Mrs. Smiley, but it wasn't easy, with everyone else pressing in for help. The officer nodded and listened. Naturally, none of us could think of her house number when he asked.

About then Evelyn's dad pushed into our circle.

"We've got an injured woman over here. Need a couple of men. She's trapped."

"Right!" The officer swung around. "Don't worry," he called to Mom over his shoulder.

We stood there and looked at each other, worrying more than ever. I could feel Mom shivering against me. The firemen had already begun searching houses, marking foundations afterward with red spray paint, but we knew for a fact they wouldn't get to Smiley's for a long time. Neither would that police officer.

"Hey, you forgot to tell him about her hearing aid," I said. "What if they call and she doesn't answer? They'll think nobody's there."

Mom looked down at Ryan, who was starting to whimper. I knew by her face that she'd made up her mind to do something.

"I'm going back," she said. "Stacey, you'll have to take the baby."

"Let *us* go back," Arthur interrupted, "the three of us. Without Ryan along, we can be there in five minutes. What could you do by yourself, anyway?"

Suddenly we were all talking at once.

"I'd be crazy to send you kids—"

"I got the boys out, Mrs. Hatch. I wouldn't let anything happen to them."

"Please, Mom? We've got two flashlights. We can get there lots faster than those firemen who have to search every house along the way."

"Absolutely not!" she kept saying.

Only after that same officer got on the bullhorn asking for volunteers and several people gathered around did she finally give in.

"Will you promise to stick together? And you're only to see to Mrs. Smiley, you hear? No detours! Stacey, you bring them right back to this corner."

She'd have kept on about how crazy it was for us to stay and not her, but by then Ryan was crying.

"The baby needs you most," Stacey said, throwing in the clincher. "Don't worry about us, Mrs. Hatch. We'll be okay."

It was all very confusing for a few minutes as we got Mom and Ryan on the bus headed for Kmart. Mom had to take a message from Stacey to Mrs. Darlington—in case she'd ended up there and not at the armory—and messages from a few others who were staying behind to volunteer help.

At the end Mom hugged us all again, right there in front of everybody boarding the bus.

"I'm really proud of you kids, you know that?"

She sniffled saying it, but she didn't cry. "Now please, *please* be careful. And stay with the others."

She gave me an extra nuzzle on the neck.

"Oh, Mom," I said, "you don't need to get all mushy."

She cuffed me one as I turned and fled.

Later On

I guess Mom expected some other volunteers to rush right off to Mrs. Smiley's with us, but that wasn't the way things worked out. The "civilians," as a Civil Defense man called them, were needed elsewhere. We didn't wait to find out where. We just took off running.

What we saw when we got to Smiley's place was really incredible. Her big old cottonwoods were still in leaf. Beyond the trees, her white frame house loomed in front of us same as always, only now it was topless. Amazingly, the walls were still standing foursquare! The front porch jutted out like the chin of a stubborn old-timer who'd simply refused to budge.

Quickly we were up on the porch, moving aside the limbs and trash that had blown onto it, all of us exclaiming over Belle Smiley's good luck.

"She was right about her new storm door," Arthur said as we walked in. "Only a couple of dents."

We didn't waste any time getting to the kitchen, where the basement stairs were.

Sure enough, the steps had collapsed under the weight of the back porch, part of which seemed to have slid in sideways, landing in a mound of rubble below.

"Mrs. Smiley . . ." we called first, taking turns, listening.

"Smiley, can you hear us?"

Our only answer was the moaning of wind as it tore through the broken windows and rattled the house.

If she was down there, she didn't hear us, or couldn't answer—one or the other.

Our next problem was getting below to find her.

After dismissing a few harebrained ideas of mine, Arthur came up with a plan. Stacey thought it sounded too dangerous, but we talked her into trying it by saying we'd go first. Arthur had read about a rescue operation in the Arctic where an Eskimo had used an upended dogsled. I couldn't quite picture what he had in mind, but Stacey and I went to work doing what he told us.

Grunting, cussing as needed, the three of us lowered Smiley's heavy kitchen table, legs up, through the stair opening until it came to rest on something solid.

I was the first one to drop down on it. With Stacey training the light on me from above, I crept down the slippery-slide slope of the table until I could grab a support post. It was easy to swing from there down to the basement floor.

Arthur made the same trip. Under his weight, however, the table slipped, and the whole thing came crashing onto the cement, barely missing me. He wasn't hurt, but that ended it for Stacey. With all the noise we were making and still no response from Mrs. Smiley, I decided she had either died of a heart attack or had turned her hearing aid to zero.

Then Stacey lowered her light to us by tying it to the strings of a smelly old mop she found somewhere. My flashlight had grown so faint we left it upstairs.

Slowly at first, Arthur shone the light all around us. There wasn't any sign of Smiley. He lighted up her old-fashioned furnace, which was spooky as anything there in the dark, with its arms reaching out in all directions. Arthur and I sniffed around it, but all we could smell was a musty basement. He next shone the light across Smiley's gleaming rows of canned fruit and tomatoes, onto pieces of old furniture she had stored everywhere. There wasn't a whole lot of room for walking, but we started out.

"Mrs. Smiley!" I bellowed several times.

Arthur shot the light around and behind everything, along the narrow little passageways we came to. It gave me the creeps, thinking we could stumble over her body without seeing it. I couldn't decide which would be worse—stumbling over it or seeing it.

I guess Arthur was thinking along those same lines. "Wouldn't this make a terrific spook alley?" he whispered, turning around.

A few seconds later I heard a really weird sound.

Arthur put on his brakes so fast I bumped into him.

"You hear that?" he said.

I nodded.

We stood there, listening, as it repeated itself twice more.

"Did you find her?" Stacey called from above, making us both jump.

"SSSHHHH!" we said together.

Arthur pointed with the light. "It's coming from over there, I think."

"Will somebody answer me?" Stacey yelled louder.

"IN A MINUTE!" Arthur boomed right in my ear.

I followed him around an old dresser, past a spidery wooden high chair, then down an aisle of storage boxes, the white beam bouncing ahead of us in the direction of the noise.

I caught my breath when we saw her. There she was, curled up on an old sofa with only her mouse-nest hair sticking out above the blanket. She wasn't dead, she was asleep! And snoring for all she was worth!

Arthur grinned at me. We started to laugh, we couldn't help it. How could *anyone* sleep through a tornado?

She made another little series of snorts—dainty this time, as if she knew we were listening.

Arthur bent double, grabbing his sides. We couldn't stop howling, either of us.

Over the sounds of wind battering the house, Stacey heard us whooping it up and thought we'd flipped.

"What's going on?" she kept yelling.

We were too weak to answer.

A little later, it was almost as funny trying to get Mrs. Smiley "out of this bloomin' cellar," as she put it.

She was being an awfully good sport but said she wasn't no mountain goat and to remember that.

We couldn't get her to try the stair-step system that Arthur rigged up under a window with a chair and a stool, though he demonstrated it could be done—with a little pull-up there at the end.

"Pull-up!" Smiley snorted. "I'm eighty-one years old, boys. Don't you think I'm better off to stay down here?"

"It's too dangerous," Arthur tried to explain. "The police said everyone had to get out because there could be explosions and fires."

"Landsakes!" she muttered. "Never thought I'd be chased off by a darned old cyclone!" She kept running her hands in and out of her sweater pockets. I could tell she was plenty nervous.

Stacey was outside the window by that time, removing broken glass from the sill with that same mop, giving us weather reports.

"Can't you guys think of something?" she said. "The rain's let up for a minute. It'll be lots easier if we can get Mrs. Smiley down to the bus before it starts again."

Suddenly Smiley brightened. "How about if we call the fire department? They'd come out for an old scaredy-cat like me."

I flashed the light at Arthur, who was rolling his eyes. We couldn't get it through her head how bad things were.

"If we fool around long enough," he said down low, "the fire department *will* be here."

Finally, though, I had an idea. We dragged the sofa she'd been sleeping on to the window and tried angling a set of old-timey bedsprings from the cushions to the wall.

Arthur and I took turns testing it, changing the angle of the springs, trying it again. It sagged a little under Arthur's weight, but it made a pretty fair ladder for someone my size.

Smiley watched, shining the light for us as we worked, predicting everything from broken bones to heart failure if she tried to climb that "monkey fence" herself.

By the time we were ready to boost her up there, Stacey had a blanket folded on the windowsill.

"We'll get you out," she kept encouraging Smiley. "I'm really strong, huh, Arthur? We can't leave you here, you know. Anything could happen." Then, as if she'd just thought of it, "Hey, I could try it first. . . . I will if you want me to."

For a second I forgot all about Smiley. Stacey looked so beautiful hanging over that windowsill, her hair whipping across her red and swollen cheek. I was beginning to think of her as a rescuing angel or something.

"Take her other arm, Dan," Stacey said in a sharp voice that brought me back to earth.

It took a little more coaxing, but we finally got Smiley up on the sofa, grasping the coils in both hands and looking scared.

"Spiderman!" Arthur whispered before I punched him.

Thank goodness for Stacey, who was hanging halfway in now, saying all the right things. I don't think Smiley would have tried it for Arthur and me alone.

The two of us stood on the sofa below, Arthur

on one side, me on the other, boosting her from behind as she started on up.

The situation suddenly struck Smiley as being very funny.

"I'm not going to believe I did this!" she said in this giggly voice as she reached for another hand-hold. "When I wake up, I'll just know I never did this." And then "Push!" she sang out.

We pushed.

We also had to take turns getting her shoes in the next spring coil up.

On she went, six inches at a time.

"Here comes Sir Edmund Hillary!" she announced better than halfway.

Arthur and I cracked up.

"Keep coming! You're almost here," cool Stacey said at the top.

Once there, Smiley paused, teetering dangerously as she tried to see out the window past Stacey. "Oh, lord, I hope the whole neighborhood isn't out there to see me kill myself."

"I'm the only one here," Stacey said, "and you're doing great!"

Stacey had a good grip on Smiley's shoulders now. "One more step ought to do it, Mrs. Smiley. Can you take one more step?"

It took all three of us, using the push-pull method, to get her through that little rectangular window. Tiny as she is, she claimed to have dropped ten pounds during the process, but the only thing she lost that we could see was a button off her old gardening sweater.

"And my dignity," she was to say later, improving the story each time she told it.

After getting her out, Arthur and I easily scrambled up those coils and out the window, we'd had so much practice.

By then, Stacey was shining the flashlight all around and under the trees so Smiley could see how our neighborhood had been devastated. The house that once stood a hefty stone's throw from Smiley's simply didn't exist anymore.

"Oh, my . . ." she said in a trembly voice, "oh, my, oh, my . . . I thought I was the only one."

Her skirt flapped noisily against her skinny bowed legs.

Nobody was laughing now.

Mrs. Smiley hung on to Stacey's arm all the way to the Darlingtons'. As we neared their place, we could see firemen searching the two or three rooms where walls had been left standing. In slickers and hard hats, they were easy to spot. Their lights criss-crossed in the dark, slicing eerily through holes in the bedroom hallway. We could hear their voices calling back and forth.

Suddenly Arthur came to life. "Hey, that's our house!"

He grabbed the light from Stacey, went crashing across the yard. He and one of the firemen talked a minute.

"All clear, move on," the fireman called to the others.

He jumped to the ground beside Arthur, and they walked around to the street side of the remains. There, in the overlapping circles made by their lights, this guy sprayed a giant red X on the Darlingtons' cement foundation.

Then the two of them came out to the street where we waited, bunched together with our backs to the wind.

"You all live around here?" he shouted.

Smiley and I gave him our names and addresses. He wrote it all down on a pad that came out of his pocket.

"Officer, please," Mrs. Smiley asked, "how bad is it?"

I could see his shoulders sag in the wash of our

light. He hesitated, slapping his huge gloves against his leg as we closed in to hear better.

"Ma'am, I wish I knew. Capital Heights, Kuester's Lake were both hit before you were. Another one touched down north of here. Patrol cars coming in from Hastings say there's been some twister action around Phillips, that's all I know."

I drew in my breath. *Not Phillips! Not the farm!*

I was strangled by fear all over again.

"You folks get out as fast as you can," he went on. "Power lines are down everywhere. Mainline gas has been shut off, but there's no way to guarantee anyone's safety if they stay in the area."

With the next jab of lightning he left us and returned to his crew. The sky grumbled all the way across and back again as I sent up one more desperate prayer. Even above the storm I could hear the racket my heart was making against my ribs.

The look on Arthur's face told me he knew what was going on in my mind. *His* dad was safe at the armory.

"Come on, Dan." He pulled me around. "Let's you and me hustle Smiley down to the bus. You can ask around, find out something, okay?"

I wanted to run after that fireman, to make him

tell me more, but already Smiley was getting a good grip on my arm.

"I'm sure lucky," she chortled at my ear, "to have such nice boys to escort me."

With a twelve-year-old escort on either side, she was practically swept off her feet. For sure we hurried her along faster than Stacey did, who had been taking the same mincey little steps as Smiley. She might be eighty-one, but she had survived with all her funnybones intact.

Mom's big bus was gone, but people had started lining up for a minibus parked in the intersection. Some of the neighbors around us were hugging each other, a few were crying. Little kids clung to their mothers' hands or hung on to their legs. I recognized a girl from school, but we were both struck with shyness.

One older guy we didn't know just stood there in the middle of the street, looking bewildered. When Arthur flipped the light on him for a second, he didn't even blink. I think he was in a state of shock.

A utility company truck pulled into the circle of vehicles as we arrived. A cop who'd been setting up flares walked over and talked to the driver. The whole scene seemed psychedelic and somehow unreal, as the flashing yellow-and-red lights turned rain-drops into streaming colored beads.

Even with so much distraction, I couldn't stop thinking about my dad and that tornado whirling toward Phillips. Who could I ask? Who would know? If only someone had a radio going!

Just then, several ladies came back to speak to Smiley. I couldn't believe it, but Ruth Pavelka from our church was actually making jokes about the ba-zaar the Presbyterians would have to cancel. Good old Ruth! Soaking wet, her hair plastered to her head, she was trying to make everyone laugh.

"I hated that quilt I was stitching from the very beginning," she told Smiley. "It just had the feel of bad luck, you know what I mean?"

By the time we four got to the head of the line, the driver was closing the doors. "Sorry," he said, "I can't jam in one more person."

Smiley's expression drooped as we were forced to step back, but not for long. An older kid in a front seat stood up and got off so she could have his place. Ruth Pavelka cheered. I didn't know the kid, but he looked about eighteen, and his sweatshirt said, "It's Hard to Be Humble When You're a Corn-husker."

The driver thanked him, then stepped down so

he could help Smiley on. Suddenly she was in no big hurry, now that her seat was reserved.

"I'd sure enough have perished if it hadn't been for you kids," she said, patting each of us in turn. "Come by for some fresh-baked cookies real soon, you hear?"

I saw Arthur and Stacey grin at each other as something of Smiley's spirit passed between them. Even I felt better. Soon, she'd said, come by *soon.*

Then we were waving good-bye and Smiley was waving back at us through the window.

The faint smell of cookies, so tantalizing seconds before, disappeared as quickly as it came. I was out on the farm with my dad. With Grandpa and Grandma . . . I was thinking of the farmhouse, which had been built during the Great Depression, without a basement. The storm cellar was a long way from the back porch, I remembered, and the doors were very hard to open.

Eleven O'clock

The few of us who couldn't get on the minibus were
herded into two police cars. The only person not
cooperating was the man we'd seen standing dazed
in the middle of the street. He was totally out of
it, just as we'd thought. We watched as two officers
helped him into the car with Ruth Pavelka, her
daughter, and the cornhusker kid.

The three of us filled the backseat of the other
cop car. Me first, Stacey in the middle, Arthur behind

the driver's seat. We were all wet and clammy and shaking like crazy, but I didn't care anymore; I wanted to get moving. I knew we'd hear some radio reports, maybe something about Phillips.

Then our driver was sliding in behind the wheel. He wiped his glasses with his handkerchief, all the while telling us his name was Kelly, joking that it was a good standard cop name and easy to remember. He could see we were nervous, I guess. Then, before starting the engine and the windshield wipers, he asked our names and we told him.

"Nine, zero, eight, four," Officer Kelly said into the mike next. "Leaving the twelve hundred block on Fonda Way with two males, one female passenger, evacuees. En route to Kmart."

The radio blasted us with noise as we took off. Arthur and I exchanged weird faces across Stacey. There were so many messages crackling back and forth we couldn't understand a word. What a garbled-up mess! The radio was going crazy.

"Are you getting any of that?" Arthur blurted out.

"Some," the officer said, glancing at us in his rearview mirror. "Heavy congestion right now."

He swung the car into the middle of the street, where we were buffeted by wind strong enough to compete with the radio. I peered out the side window through water streaks. Total blackness. Only straight in front of the headlights could we see that this part of Fonda Way was in much better shape than where we lived.

I strained to pick up some information from the radio. Now and then, something that made sense came through before the static took over.

Engine six responding. I caught that much. Most of what I was hearing was the sounds of panic—the sounds of disaster, I realized with a shudder.

. . . *strong odor of gas . . . two occupants . . .* Another barrage of static. *Pagoda Lounge.*

Talk piling on top of talk. Layers and layers of messages, enough noise and confusion to bruise your ears, but not one word about Phillips.

Squad four needs fuel. . . . Dodge School . . . Hey, that was my school this year! Mine and Arthur's.

Brrraaaak! . . . en route to pick up body . . .

Kelly turned down the volume a little.

I gave up listening and stared at the blackness outside the window, concentrating on the little warm spot I had inside me: Mom and Ryan. I'd be with them soon. I could hardly wait. Mom wouldn't be afraid to ask questions. She'd find out what was happening in Phillips.

I tried picturing them inside that sprawling Kmart

store. At least there would be diapers and warm clothes for Ryan. I'd seen their boxes of Pampers stacked clear to the ceiling once. And there would be food.

But what if I couldn't find them? What if there was such a crowd of people there I couldn't find my mom? I'd been lost once in Kmart, and just remembering it made my heart beat faster. They'd had to announce me on the loudspeaker: "Two-year-old boy wearing shorts and a striped T-shirt." Naturally, I was crying when Mom got to me, but not for the reason they thought. I was *three*! I had held up three fingers, and that lady said I was two.

Attacked by a high-pitched radio whine, I sat up and paid attention again. I didn't know exactly where we were, but the street we were on now hadn't been disturbed at all except for some flooding. We had to slow down going through the water, which splashed high alongside the car. I can't tell you how good it felt to see those rows of neat little houses in our headlights, facing each other across the street the way houses are supposed to. No debris, no upended trees. Everything nice and orderly.

Then it struck me—there weren't any lights, anywhere, except ours. We might as well have been out in the middle of the prairie. I swallowed into a dry throat. That meant there wouldn't be any lights at the Kmart, either.

"Where are your parents?" the policeman shouted back, startling me.

Stacey leaned forward and explained. When she finished, well, that's when I tried to ask about the tornado sighted near Phillips, but I guess he couldn't hear my voice over everything else.

"Keep your fingers crossed," he said over his shoulder a minute later. "We'll try for the Kmart, but we may not get through."

"How come?" Arthur asked.

Officer Kelly removed his hat, shook off the drops, stuck it back on. For a minute I thought he hadn't heard Arthur, either.

"South Locust is gone," he said finally. "Wiped out."

Stacey's hands flew to cover her mouth.

Arthur shot forward on the back seat. "Taco John's?" he squeaked.

"Taco John's and everything else," he said, "both sides of the street."

I couldn't believe it. All those stores and restaurants? Dreisbach's? Ramada Inn? The supermarket? South Locust was the main drag at our end of Grand

Island, a big, broad street with buildings strong as fortresses.

He went on. "The place looks like a bombing range. Somehow, Kmart escaped the worst of it. "

"Like Smiley's, huh, Dan?" Arthur said.

"So Kmart's now the evacuation center. . . . Hold it!" Officer Kelly said suddenly, bending to the radio.

We all shut up.

. . . struck a second time . . .

What? What was struck a second time? What were they saying?

Squad four out of gas north of the interchange.
Say it again! *What* was struck?

. . . all rescue units . . . one four zero one to fire captain . . . Hastings Civil Defense . . .

I was straining to sift out the words. Then *children trapped* and *Meves Bowl* came through clear as anything. Someone was repeating it over and over. They were calling all rescue units to Meves Bowl. *Meves!* Aunt Goldie! That's where—

Suddenly our driver jammed on the brakes, flipped a U-ie that threw Arthur and Stacey hard against me. He had us going the other way before we knew what was happening. I figured we were heading back to the bowling alley until I saw the terror on Kelly's face.

"Get down!" he shouted. "NOW!"

Our headlights—and those of the car coming at us—were swallowed by the blackness.

"Stay down!" he ordered as our siren revved to full blast. WAH, WAH, WAH, WAH, WAH! Kelly swung the car around, blocking the one coming toward us. By then we were down between the seats on top of each other.

I heard the other car's brakes as it spun around. Then the noise from behind us, the same terrifying roar, rising and falling in our ears above the siren.

Oh, God, please, God!

The patrol car jerked forward. It stopped! . . . We began to bounce. . . . Up and down, side to side. Leaping forward and bouncing at the same time. . . . Stacey's fingers dug into my shoulders. My head banged against the door with every lurch. I bit my tongue so hard I could taste blood.

"I've got it floorboarded," Kelly shouted, "but we're not moving!"

What I heard next was this frantic voice on the radio. No badge numbers or ten-fours or anything, just this voice laced with panic: *Kelly, get the hell out of there!*

"I'm trying!" he cried.

Sure enough, the explosion came next. The

windshield popped and threw glass all over us. At the same time, miraculously, the patrol car lurched forward. I felt us accelerating, rocking from side to side, speeding away from the tornado sound. I wanted to cry, I was so relieved. My eyes were shut tight, but tears were coming out just the same.

"My God, my God!" Kelly's voice rang out, wobbly with fear. "Somebody up there's crazy about us! That was too close!"

Stacey's elbow dug into my back as she straightened to sit up. I opened my eyes, shook off the glass.

"You kids okay?"

I scrambled to my knees. When Kelly turned on the inside light to check the backseat, I noticed his glasses were shattered right out of their frames.

We all talked at once. Babbling was what it was. We were worse than the radio.

Seconds later, Kelly had the siren off and was on the mike again. "Tornado on the ground," he said, giving location and time. "Just missed us. No assessment of damage possible." Then he repeated it in a voice that was still several pitches above normal.

"Forget Kmart," he said afterward, "we're taking her in to headquarters."

All I wanted was to get out of there in one piece.

Then I noticed Kelly wasn't driving too straight.

He had let up on the gas. Pretty soon he was hunched forward over the wheel, pulling his hat low over his face.

"Dan!" he called.

"Yeah?"

"Come on up here."

I didn't ask questions. I brushed glass off the back of the seat and climbed over.

"Ever steered before?"

It suddenly dawned on me. He couldn't see! I put one hand on the wheel. "Yeah, lots of times."

"I took some glass. I'm losing my vision."

He moved over against the door so I could get the feel of steering with both hands. I couldn't see a whole lot either, with the rain driving right in on us.

"You know how to get to headquarters?"

My stomach flopped. I didn't. I was terrible on the downtown streets. I knew *about* . . .

"I know," Stacey spoke up.

"Me, too," said Arthur. "We go right by, taking Dad to the armory."

Officer Kelly was blinking now and grimacing. I figured he must be hurting a lot because he'd slowed way down.

"You want me to drive?" I asked, braver than I

felt. I was keeping her steady, right down the middle, but then, nobody was out on the streets anyway. "Grandpa lets me drive the tractor all the time."

He let up on the accelerator and kind of helped me ease into the curb, putting the gearshift on park.

"Go to it, Dan," he said. "I can't see a thing."

"Nine zero eight four . . . nine zero eight four," he said into the mike. "Reporting injury affecting my eyesight . . . returning to headquarters assisted by minor male passenger."

Minor male passenger! That's me, Dan Hatch! I was having chills on top of chills.

He repeated his message, then we switched places. He was really in trouble, I could tell, but he was still thinking *safety.* He got the flashers going and put the siren on again.

"We'll be approaching from the north now," he shouted, "so turn left here, hit Pine, then head south."

"Okay," I answered.

I moved the gearshift into drive and eased my foot off the brake. My hands were shaking like anything, but we started up smooth as syrup.

"Keep her under the speed limit, pal" was the only instruction he had to give me.

I wished with all my heart that Dad could have

seen me driving that old police car down Pine Street to the station house. Next to wanting to see him, I wanted him to see me.

Mom would have keeled over. Not Dad. He and I . . . we were born on wheels, he once told me. Even with the rain and bits of glass spitting into my face, driving came as natural to me that night as breathing.

The only embarrassing part was hitting the curb too hard when we parked in front of the orange-brick Public Safety Center.

Midnight

We walked into the police station through double glass doors into a big open space the size of a classroom. Officer Kelly, his hands on my shoulder and Arthur's, steered us left toward a sign that said "Sheriff's Department." I could tell by his grip he couldn't see worth a darn anymore.

When the policewoman behind the counter looked up and saw him, she practically threw her phone down on the desk. "Kelly, my God! Angie, get a deputy out here—"

In that glaring overhead light he looked pretty terrible. Cuts were showing up all over his face— red lines dotted with pinpoints of blood—and his eyes behind the empty frames had watered clean down on his cheeks.

"I've taken some glass in my eyes," he said calmly. "Can someone tend to these kids?"

In two seconds a deputy was around from behind the counter, taking Kelly's arm. Someone else rushed out of an office. Suddenly we were surrounded by cops.

"How bad is it? Can you see?"

He tossed his car keys onto the counter. "I can't see much."

"Angie, let the hospital know we're coming—"

Someone took off his glasses. We stepped aside to let the others in around him.

"You maniac," we heard the deputy say as he started off with Kelly, "out there chasing tornadoes!"

We watched as they hustled him through an inside door. I felt a little silly waving at his back when he couldn't see me, but I did it anyway. It was awful, not being able to tell him thanks or good-bye.

Even after Kelly left, the place was a zoo. Phones were ringing nonstop. From somewhere in the back ground we could hear the massive congestion of a police radio piling up messages. Cops and people in regular clothes were in and out of offices, shouting to each other, everyone hyper.

Finally, the same policewoman who had helped Kelly came over to where we were standing at the long counter. "So you kids need shelter," she said.

I needed to find out if my dad was alive, that's what I needed.

"Kelly said you're separated from two sets of parents, is that right?"

We nodded.

"Hold on." She went back to her desk and got on the intercom with someone. "Mildred, is there room in that women's section? Yes, I have three teenagers here." I straightened, being mistaken for a teenager.

She called someone else on the intercom, after which this heavyset man in tan work clothes came out and glowered at us.

I looked down at myself, then at Arthur. We really were a sight. My jeans were filthy, torn on both legs. Quickly I wiped my face on the bottom of my shirt. Stacey didn't look much better in her oversize Levi's jacket and faded cutoffs.

"He'll take you upstairs," the police lady said.

Upstairs? What for?

"Can you tell me something first?" I heard myself

ask. "Has Phillips . . . we heard . . . did Phillips get hit by a tornado?"

"I wouldn't know. One was sighted near Hansen, I guess. People are spotting tornadoes everywhere on a night like this."

"We've been in two of them," Arthur told her.

"Is that all?" she said sarcastically. "There've been *dozens!*"

I felt like screaming at her. I knew she was upset, but she was making me feel exactly like a prisoner. Don't twelve-year-old kids have rights? I wanted to ask about Meves Bowl, too, but I lost my nerve.

On our way up the stairs, the jailor—or whatever he was—said he was taking us to the women's section: "Since there aren't any female prisoners tonight."

He led us into a carpeted room with very plain walls. There were two couches and some chairs, a table full of magazines. A policewoman was sitting on the arm of a chair talking to some people and writing stuff down on a clipboard.

The jailor pointed to a narrow open bedroom jutting off the main room. "You kids can have that unit," he said.

Two identical bedrooms on the other side were already occupied. I could hear a baby fussing over there, which made me want to be with Mom and Ryan more than ever.

The woman in the brown uniform looked up and smiled. "I'm Mrs. Minetti, the matron here. Sit down. I'll be right with you."

"Are we in jail?" I whispered to Stacey after the man left.

"The women's section . . . that's what he said."

It was pretty nice, if you asked me. I couldn't see bars anywhere.

The three of us sat down on the couch opposite the matron and stared at the other disaster victims, who were all wet and stringy-haired like us. A white-faced girl about Ronnie Vae's age stared back. She had a bandage on her arm. Two smaller kids were barefoot and shivering, wearing p.j.'s that stuck to their skin. Their mother wore a mud-splattered bathrobe minus the belt.

"We thought the storm had blown over," this lady was telling the matron, "but when Dave went outside to see if things were letting up, it knocked him flat on his face. He *crawled* back to the trailer. God in heaven, when it hit . . ." She couldn't finish.

"Our trailer was one of those big double jobs," her husband went on, "but that tornado flipped us over like a cardboard box, dragged us thirty feet."

His hands shook so bad he could hardly get a drag on his cigarette.

"When did you start to smell the gas?" Mrs. Minetti asked.

"Right after. It was terrible. . . . *Overpowering!*"

"All up and down Sycamore . . ."

Though the women's section was plenty warm, I found myself getting chills on my arms.

"It was the gas that got us out, too," the other lady said, jouncing the baby on her shoulder as she came out of a bedroom unit. The little boy who clung to her jeans pocket studied us with huge uncertain eyes.

When the adults started talking to each other, we learned that the second family had lost their house in Capital Heights and been brought in just ahead of us by a deputy sheriff.

"Everything's gone," a man said, shaking his head. Then, sadly, "Even the dog . . . yeah . . . and we happened to see her."

He shouldn't have mentioned the dog, because it set his older kid to crying. The father lifted his big boy and held him close to muffle the sobs. The dad wanted to cry, too, I could tell. I had to look away. I never wanted to see Minerva dead!

A little later, Mrs. Minetti took us into the room

with the two cots, where she asked our names and what had happened. She gave us a scratchy army blanket, too, "just in case." I liked her. She had brown hair like Mom's and friendly eyes. I was glad she was in charge and not that other policewoman. There was plainly nothing else to be glad about, getting stuck in a jail, not knowing if my dad was dead or alive.

When Arthur went off to the john, Stacey and I sat there on the two cots and looked at each other. I was so tired, I just wanted to fall over and go to sleep. Then Stacey smiled, which made me smile because her face went all crooked on one side from the swelling.

"You okay, Dan?"

"Yeah."

She bounced a little on the striped mattress, which was covered with plastic. Testing it, I guess.

"Ever think you'd end up in jail?" she asked. She stood and tried to look out the high window.

"How come they put us in here?" I blurted out suddenly. "How are we going to know what's happening?" I couldn't get Dad off my mind. What if he'd driven straight into that tornado on South Locust? We always came home from Phillips that way.

Stacey didn't answer, but when she sat down again

it was right next to me. I was hoping she'd put her arm around me the way she'd done earlier, but she didn't. She was too busy picking dried blood off her leg.

"Think of it this way, Dan. Would you rather sleep here where it's nice and warm or on the floor at Kmart?"

"Kmart!" I said without batting an eye.

"Okay, *okay*!" Stacey sighed as she took off her dad's jacket.

When I pointed out that one sleeve of her blouse was ripped, she finished it off, then slipped the cuff end over her hand. She rolled up the other sleeve to match. I had to laugh when she told me uneven sleeves were going to be the new style in Grand Island.

Stacey took her turn in the john next. Arthur and I pulled a bed to the window and climbed up, calling each other "jailbird" and "juvenile offender," trading elbow digs as we tried to see out.

The sky overhead was black as ever, though the rain had let up. There were no city lights at all. Only the parking areas around the Public Safety Center were ablaze.

"They have their own generator," Arthur told me, as if I hadn't figured that out already.

119

Just then a siren started up below, making me think of Kelly again. I'd never be able to sleep in that jail, edgy as I was about everything.

Arthur was getting edgy, too, I guess. Several times he tried to open the window before we jumped down, but he couldn't. Making a desperate face, Arthur pulled his T-shirt up above his belly and started fanning himself. "It's too hot in this place. Can't we get any air?"

Stacey was on her way back and heard us grumbling.

"Will you two shut up? Do you know how lucky we are? We're *alive* . . . and our families are alive!"

"Maybe," I muttered.

"Just shut up, both of you."

Arthur wasn't about to. "I'm scared, you big smart ass!" he yelled suddenly, giving her a shove. "You don't have brains enough to be scared. There are nine of us, remember? How are we going to live?"

Stacey backed off. "There are going to be ten of us soon," she said coolly.

Arthur stared. It was so quiet in that women's section right then, you could have heard a cockroach sneeze.

"Mama's *pregnant?*"

"Don't broadcast it," Stacey whispered. "She

doesn't want the whole world to know yet."

Arthur grinned at me, everything else forgotten. "Maybe we'll get a boy . . . like Ryan. No lie, Stacey, is she really?"

Stacey nodded gravely.

Arthur once told me their family believed babies were God's jewels. I also knew he was tired of being surrounded by females.

"Come on, let's push these cots together," Stacey said, all sweet and motherly again. "We'll have to sleep crosswise."

We had just stretched out to see if we'd fit when Mrs. Minetti came back in with some trays of food.

"It's all I could find," she apologized to everybody. "You kids will just have to pretend you're at the A&W."

I wasn't going to do *that*. Didn't she know the A&W was in splinters like everything else on South Locust?

We sat down on the floor under the window, behind the beds where it was cooler and more private. "Our midnight snack," as Stacey called it, amounted to seven graham crackers each, with one left over, and three cans of cold 7-Up. I have to admit that jail food tasted better than anything I'd ever had at the A&W.

"I'm needed down below," Mrs. Minetti announced before she left, "so I'm turning the lights off in these bedroom units. You all try to get some sleep. You'll need it."

Everyone thanked her. Everyone except the baby, that is, who kept on crying, even with a graham cracker in each fist. I figured the kid must be teething, like Ryan.

"I wonder why that tornado happened to us," Arthur said, sitting there beside me. "Why didn't it hit Lincoln or Kearney . . . or someplace in Iowa?"

Stacey leaned forward to brush the crumbs off her shirt front, all the time watching the lady with the baby.

Arthur scooted closer. "You know what?" he said.

"What?" I answered absently.

I was just finishing my last cracker, wondering how long it would take Stacey to go help with that crying baby. I was feeling sorry for the poor mother myself and only halfway paying attention to Arthur when Stacey set her 7-Up down on the tray.

"Be back in a minute," she said.

"Hey!" Arthur banged on my leg until I turned to face him. "Listen, Dan, this is important."

"Yeah?"

"You know that bull-roarer I made?"

I nodded.

"You know what the Hopi Indians believe?"

My eyes were back on Stacey. Sure enough, the lady was letting her take the baby.

"Dan, what if *I* caused that tornado?" he whispered in a hoarse voice.

"What are you talking about?"

"The *bull-roarer*! The Hopi Indians won't let their kids play with bull-roarers inside. Not in the spring, leastways. You know that roaring sound they make?"

I nodded.

"That sound is supposed to bring on the whirlwind—death and destruction and all that. I knew about it, but I swung the bull-roarer anyway. Remember your Aunt Goldie's place? It was ripped apart worse than anybody's."

"Arthur! Bull-roarers don't cause tornadoes!" He was lots smarter than me. How could he even think that?

"Why us, then? Grand Island, Nebraska, the All-American City. Why *our* neighborhood?"

"There were tornadoes spinning down all over," I reminded him.

He leaned back against the wall and pressed his lips together. I guess I was making him mad. I leaned back, too, and sucked on the edge of my 7-Up can.

In spite of the heat in there, goose bumps began to finger my scalp. Was it any different . . . what *I'd* been thinking? We both knew about tornadoes—storm cells and squall lines and all that. Then why had I been thinking the same way as Arthur? Only with me it wasn't some stupid bull-roarer, it was Ryan. It was all those times I'd wished Ryan out of existence. I'd been sick of him from the day he was born.

I squeezed my can flat with both hands, pushing the air out of my lungs at the same time. If anyone was being punished with a tornado, I was. I was the one who had resented a helpless baby, my own flesh and blood. I wondered now how I could have felt that way about him.

"Arthur," I spoke up, determined to straighten him out, "that tornado wasn't anybody's fault."

"Don't you think I know that?"

"But you just said—"

"I know what I said." He got to his feet, grinning. "C'mon, let's pick our spots before Stacey comes back. She's a real bed hog."

Arthur took off his shoes and settled himself at one end, stretching across the two cots. It took me longer, pulling off one water-logged sock after the other, then rolling up the muddied bottoms of my jeans. I took my time inspecting my feet, which looked like prehistoric monsters, they were so wrinkled and gray.

By the time I was ready to lie down, Arthur was breathing hard. It took all of three minutes for him to fall asleep.

With Arthur unconscious beside me, I turned my head so I could see what was going on in the big room. The men had propped open the door and were standing near the entrance, smoking and talking in low voices. The mother in the opposite bedroom unit was washing her kids with a cloth that looked like the cuff end of Stacey's sleeve. The girl with the bandaged arm lay on one of the sofas, very still, her dark eyes open. I wondered if I'd ever seen her at Dodge Elementary, but I didn't think I had.

Stacey was now playing peekaboo with the baby, hiding behind the overstuffed chair, then popping out with these squeaky sounds that made the little kid laugh. The baby's mother had her hands full trying to get her other one to sleep.

I pulled my knees up trying to get comfortable, but no matter how I arranged myself, one cut or another stuck to the plastic. I finally gave up and closed my eyes.

I couldn't think about my dad or Grandpa and Grandma. It made me too nervous. I concentrated on Mom and Ryan instead, wondering what they'd be doing in that big old store. Maybe the Kmart people had opened the cafeteria and were making pizza for everyone. I had a really crazy thought next. What if the Kmart was doomed to be our summer home? That might not be too bad! I pictured the video games and the oversize toy department, the aisle of kitchen things Mom always had to look at. Kmart would be a lot more interesting a place to live than the armory. Then I remembered the armory had a basketball court, and I couldn't decide which would be better.

I opened my eyes to check on Stacey. Why would she rather count some strange baby's toes than finish drinking her 7-Up? Wasn't she ever coming back?

I finally got up and went to the bathroom. I splashed my face and arms, took a big drink, then watched as the water pressure fell off right before my eyes. The stream reduced to a trickle, then stopped. I turned the faucet off, waited, tried it again. Nothing but drips.

"The water's quit," I whispered to Stacey when I got back to the main room. The baby had fallen asleep in the big chair and Stacey was sitting on the floor, patting its grubby-looking undershirt. She gave me a grim look, sent me to tell the two mothers, who thanked me for the bad news.

After that Stacey and I went back to our "cell," where she finished her drink.

"What does it mean when the pressure dies down like that?" I asked.

"I don't know. I guess it means we're in trouble. "I mean . . . even *more* trouble."

There was plenty of water outside: It was raining again. Mixed with hail, it tapped sharply against the window, pelted the roof over our heads. What was to keep those tornadoes from coming back and flattening the Public Safety Center the way they'd flattened our houses and all those big buildings on South Locust?

"I'll never be able to sleep," I told Stacey.

"Me neither," she said, "but we gotta try."

We lay down across the cots, facing each other in the half-dark, hardly a foot between us. Having her there made me feel much better, I have to admit. I figured I could spend a whole lifetime lying that way next to Stacey and not be unhappy about it.

"My face is really a mess, huh?" she whispered.

I shook my head against the plastic. Even black and blue, she looked terrific to me.

We closed our eyes. When I opened mine again, Stacey was looking at me.

"Don't be worried, Danny."

"I can't help it."

"You know something? Mama quotes Scripture when she gets upset. Says it's like taking a tranquilizer."

"Wish I knew some Scripture," I said, which was only half true.

"You know 'The Lord is my shepherd,' don't you?"

"Everybody knows that."

"Okay, so . . . here, Dan . . . we have to hold hands. Anyway, this is how we do it at home."

I felt kind of funny about Stacey holding my hand, which was all sweaty and hot, but then it didn't matter after all because so was hers.

"Now, like Mama says, you have to make a picture in your mind to go with every line we say, or it won't work. Want to try it?"

I nodded.

"The Lord is my shepherd." She stopped there. "Are you getting a picture?"

"Yeah." I was! I was seeing a shepherd, plain as anything.

"So what's he wearing?"

"Uh . . . sandals. And a long robe."

"Does he have a cloth thing on his head?"

"He does now." I described it for her. It was wheat colored, with a red border design. Something like a sweatband held it in place.

"Hey, great, Danny!" Stacey squeezed my hand and smiled her weird smile.

We went on through the green pastures and the still waters. I saw the lambs, all soft and fluffy. I heard them bleat for their mothers. We hadn't come to the "valley of the shadow of death" or "my cup runneth over" when all the lights in the place went out.

We sat straight up. Stacey rushed to the window, jumped a few times.

"They're off down below, too," she said.

We automatically grabbed hands when she came back. I couldn't believe it, but hers had already turned cold.

In the big room one of the men struck a match. The light drew the parents together like a magnet. In the brief flickering we could see the girl on the sofa was sitting up, too.

"Auxiliary power's gone," one of the men said. "Must have blown the generator."

"Dan," Stacey whispered, her voice suddenly grown quavery, "this really scares me."

129

"It doesn't scare me," I lied right in my teeth. "I'm not scared at all."

I held her hand tight, marveling that it was exactly the same size as mine, and squeezed my eyes shut against the terrifying dark. I started in again on the Twenty-third Psalm, only to myself this time. Funny how that shepherd, who sure enough had Jesus' face to start with, was looking more and more like my own dad.

The next thing I knew I was being jolted awake by the thundering roar of helicopters going right over our heads.

Early Morning

It was scarcely daylight when the National Guard choppers made their first overview of the city. Though we didn't know it at the time, they were carrying the mayor, the police chief, the city engineer, and two civil defense chiefs—all of them stunned to silence by what they saw.

One of the officials was so shocked, he later reported he hadn't even heard the sound of the rotors. "That was the quietest helicopter ride I ever took," he said.

All we knew for sure in our cramped little jail cell was that it was morning and we wanted out of there.

We didn't wait to ask permission. We just went ahead and used the john, which sure enough had stopped flushing, then tiptoed out.

Down below, Mrs. Minetti gave us dimes for the public phone so we could try to reach Grandma Hatch and the armory, but we struck out on both.

"Some calls are getting through," she told us, "but if the lines are down you won't get anything more than a busy signal."

She had changed out of her uniform into slacks and was about to leave for the nearby town of Doniphan, where she lived. When she heard us talking among ourselves about walking to Kmart and the armory, she asked the policewoman at the desk if she shouldn't just drive us in her car.

"If we can't get through, I'll take them home with me," she said.

I hoped not, though I could see she halfway liked the idea.

Before we knew it, she was herding us toward the same double glass doors we'd walked through five or six hours earlier.

Outside, dawn showed us a gray and sodden world.

It didn't look as if the sun would rise or set on any-body that fourth day of June.

I had always wondered what Grandpa meant when he said he can smell tornado weather. I've always been able to feel it: My clothes never really dry out. The humidity that morning must have been 90 percent. Or maybe it wasn't the weather right then, maybe it was me. Maybe I was a lot more worried than I knew. For whatever reason—humid-ity or nerves—I found that air heavy and musty and very hard to breathe. I finally knew what Grandpa was talking about.

I can't remember much about going to the armory, except that we got through without any trouble. In-side, there were people everywhere, asleep on cots or just waking up. Stacey and Arthur led us straight past the gym and down a dark hall to their dad's office. That's where we found Mr. Darlington, look-ing really hashed, yelling at some operator on the phone.

I'll never forget the expression on his face when he saw us. He grabbed up his kids as if they were featherweights, one in each arm, kissing and hugging them like crazy. We couldn't stop smiling, any of us. Mr. Darlington hugged me, too, until I thought my ribs would crack. He's a great big man, someone who doesn't know his own strength when it comes to a welterweight like me.

"Where *were* you?" he asked. "I got through to Dan's place, searched everywhere. The Millers told me they saw you leaving—that's all I had to go on."

Mrs. Minetti explained about the jail, with the rest of us adding our two bits' worth. Then he sent Stacey and Arthur off to find the rest of their family. No, he said, he hadn't seen my dad or Aunt Goldie, either one. I just stood there, feeling worse by the minute, as he and Mrs. Minetti went on talking.

We'd no sooner turned to leave than back came Arthur to smack me a couple of good ones on the arm, finishing off what his dad had begun.

"See you, Hatch," he said, letting me grab him around the neck before he took off again. He was going to see more of me than ever in the days ahead, but neither of us knew it then.

In no time at all Mrs. Minetti and I were back in her Dodge en route to Kmart.

I kept my fingers crossed all the way to Highway 34, then nearly died when the National Guard patrol wouldn't let us pass. Only after Minetti produced her official I.D. did he wave us on around the other traffic trying to enter the city.

"Approaching from this direction," she told me, "we might just make it."

When we got to South Locust and saw what loomed ahead of us in that early light, we changed our minds. The street was jammed with bulldozers, trucks, emergency vehicles, National Guardsmen on foot. An ambulance was trying to get through behind a piece of heavy equipment, wailing and wailing without making any headway. The familiar skyline was gone. Once-sturdy buildings were now so many layers of rubble. The sight of those groaning bulldozers pushing the debris into piles made me sick to my stomach.

I remembered that my dad would come in this way from Phillips. *If* he came in. . . . What would he think, seeing all this? What would he think had happened to us?

We tried another way, but had to turn back because of downed wires and water. The next two streets were blockaded as well. Finally, Mrs. Minetti pulled to the curb and parked. She looked at me a long time, shaking her head. I knew what she was going to say.

"I know you don't want to, but you'll have to come home with me . . . or let me take you back to the armory. Believe me, your mother wouldn't want you here. It's a war zone!"

"Can't I just walk to the Kmart?" I begged her. "It's not that far now. You don't know how my mom worries when she doesn't know where I am."

"Oh, Dan." Her eyes filled up. "I can't just leave you here."

I already had the door open, glad she wasn't trying to stop me.

"I'll be okay, honest!"

"Wait—" She reached for me, all right, but by then I was free.

I waved at her and ran, tears streaming down my face. I don't know why I was crying, but I was. Crying as hard as I ever had, crying and running. Around the barricade, splashing through the low places, leaping over the kindling-wood remains of somebody's house, dodging wires that draped crazily everywhere. I never stopped and I never looked back.

I'm sure it wasn't yet seven by the time I got to the 1600 block on Locust and spotted the Kmart, but everyone else seemed to have beat me. The parking lot was overflowing. There were news vans, guys with TV cameras, ambulances and fire trucks and National Guard jeeps everywhere. Besides the rumbling engines, sounds of walkie-talkies and CBs and people shouting orders came at me from all sides.

I skirted along the edge of the parking lot, passing the Salvation Army van, the medics, and a row of chemical toilets to reach the store itself. My heart was pounding like crazy, but I didn't get there soon enough after all. A guy wearing a hard hat stopped me.

"Hey, son, don't go in there!" he yelled at me.

I whirled around. "My mom's here. I want to see her!"

He left the small loader he was riding and came over.

"This is the official operations center. It's the CP now—the Command Post. Civilians are all gone."

"They brought her here on a school bus," I cried breathlessly, starting to shake, starting to get mad.

"Evacuated everyone during the night. Water's an inch deep in there, too much damage." He started off.

I put my face to the glass door, trying to look in, but he saw me.

"Don't go in there now, you hear me?"

I backed away.

"Where'd they take everybody?" I called after him.

"All over. The armory, Barr Junior High, churches"—he flung out his arm—"everywhere. You'll have to make the rounds."

The armory! I had good reason to cry now.

I walked away so he wouldn't yell at me again,

then sat down on the curb trying to decide what to do. There I was, smack-dab in the middle of the CP, and I was worse off than ever.

The parking lot blurred in front of my eyes.

Don't get mad, I told myself, what's the use? And don't be a crybaby either. Just figure things out. You drove a police cruiser last night, remember? You can do whatever you have to!

I wiped my face on my sleeve and took some deep breaths, trying to decide where Dad would go to look for us. He'd go home first. Then, after that . . . to the armory? If Mom was at the armory, sooner or later she'd run into the Darlingtons and they would tell her I was okay. Maybe I should go home, too. The armory was too far away.

I looked up. Colors had grown brighter. Day was coming on fast. I noticed a Red Cross van that I hadn't seen before. I saw the first-aid station I'd zoomed right by, and the medics loading an ambulance. They were sloshing around in water that was ankle deep in places. About then, a police car limped into the parking lot with its left rear tire flap-flap-flapping against the wet cement, a sight that would have cracked me up any other time.

I was beginning to feel like a casualty myself, though I could see there was no place here for ordinary survivors like me. A kid who can't find his parents isn't very high on the priority list.

I stood up, stuffed my shirt in my jeans. I knew I could get back home, and if I crossed Fonner Park it wouldn't be that long a walk. The scary part was thinking what there was to go back to. Not even Minerva—I knew it in my bones—not even my cat would be there. But home base is home base, no matter how much it's been torn up.

Just then a whiff of coffee drifted toward me from the Salvation Army van. What a good smell! It was identical to what came out of our coffee maker every morning of my life, but I'd never thought about it before. Now I was thinking about it. Dad says he doesn't wake up until he's had a cup of brew. I guess the coffee was waking me up, too, but in another way. It gave me hope—even that thin little whiff I was getting—that things would be normal again.

It was while cutting through the vast cement parking area of the racetrack, wondering why Fonner Park had so little damage, that I heard the sound of a truck accelerating somewhere behind me. Two cars had already passed me. People were discovering they could get through this way. I'd been jogging and walking by turns, sailing over the few branches that were down, half wishing I'd asked those Salvation Army ladies for a sandwich. Suddenly, the sound of that five-liter engine behind me registered in my brain. It was my dad's pickup! Furthermore, I *knew*—some spinal signal told me—that he was driving.

By the time he reached me, by the time they reached me—Mom and Dad and Ryan—I was jumping up and down and yelling.

The pickup was still rolling when Dad leaped out of that driver's seat and lifted me off my feet. Mom was out next, her arms around us both with Ryan squished in the middle. The dance we did right there at the Fonner Park Racetrack could no way be choreographed. Even by Aunt Goldie, who claimed she'd had two years of training in the East.

We went on home from there, driving slow, through streets that were still being cleared. A tornado had been on the ground near Phillips, but, thank God, it had missed the farm.

"Flooding is going to be your grandpa's worst problem," Dad told us. "The irrigation pivots are standing in a lake right now."

Then I learned how Dad had finally made his way to the house around one-fifteen, how he'd spent the next desperate hours trying to find the rest of us.

About four-thirty or so he'd discovered Mom at the Presbyterian church, where she and Ryan and Smiley were sleeping on a rug in the minister's study.

"You kids were well hidden in that jail," Dad said after I told him about us. "Everyone else was crowded into that underground shelter. I was there twice looking for you and your mother."

He'd also gone to the armory, Stolley Park School, Civil Defense headquarters, and two hospitals.

When he finally found Mom at the church, it was Smiley who tried to convince him we'd be all right.

"Don't you worry none about those kids," she'd said. "They're sly as foxes, those three. Mark my word, they're holed up somewhere just waiting for daybreak."

I had to grin when Dad told me that.

And then we were turning onto Sand Crane Drive and I wanted to close my eyes in the worst way.

The nightmare was true, I knew it. I'd braced myself for it. But by daylight everything was worse than I expected.

Dad angled the truck at the curb in front of our place and cut the engine. Nobody made a move to get out. We just sat there. I leaned into Mom, toward

Ryan, who was bent on exploring my ear.

Dad finally broke the silence.

"We'll be living on the farm awhile," he said, in a voice scratchy as sandpaper.

As Remembered
One Year Later

I guess we were lucky that Grandma still had a house. And a table—one that pulled out to seat six extra people.

The Darlingtons, being such a big family, were forced to split up after the tornado. Stacey moved in with her friend Evelyn; Arthur spent most of the summer with me on the farm. Ronnie Vae, who didn't eat or speak for three days after being thrown into the Winegars' bushes, ended up in California visiting her cousins. They said she wouldn't shut up once she got there.

Every night on the farm, after a back-breaking day's work in Grand Island, Arthur and I konked out on Grandma's sun porch. If the mosquitoes weren't too bad, we carried our mattress outside and slept under the stars. One rainy, windy night the whole bunch of us took shelter in the storm cellar with the spiders and the mice. We were all pretty nervous, though Grandpa's dog, Princess Fleabag, was the biggest coward down there, shivering and howling when the wind reached a certain pitch. Even with my arms around her she wouldn't calm down.

"I may just sell out and go to Arizona!" Grandpa said in disgust as he lit the kerosene lantern for us. Nobody believed him. He was third generation on that farm, had seen hay straws driven through trees before. He wouldn't pull up his roots any more than we would.

As it turned out, nearly everybody who lost a home did the same as the Darlingtons and the Hatches. "What else can we do," Dad said to Grandpa, "but clean up and start over?"

Thank goodness for insurance money and the promise of government loans! The new house could be built squarely on the foundation of the original one, and Mom would get to choose all her favorite colors when it came time to decorate.

Aunt Goldie was one of the few who decided not to rebuild. She was still so spacey from her tornado experience that she preferred getting an apartment closer to town, where there were lots of people around. That was okay with Arthur and me. It was a great consolation, knowing those craft classes had gone with the wind!

Though we didn't know it for several days, Aunt Goldie had sure enough been among the unlucky ones trapped at Meves Bowl the night of the twisters. Except for hiding in the ladies' room with the others when the huge steel beams tore loose, she couldn't remember much of anything. Two days later, she came to herself in a motel in Omaha—without her purse, a change of clothes, her toothbrush or anything. She tried then to get a message to us, but went to pieces again when a telephone operator told her Grand Island had been "sealed off" to the outside world.

Naturally, Mom had been beside herself with worry all that time. Though we'd alerted police and rescue people, there was no way of knowing in all the confusion if anyone was really looking for missing persons.

It was Friday of that week when a Red Cross lady

drove Aunt Goldie out to the farm. None of us asked questions. Not then. She was too shaky and confused, and we were too glad to see her. Grandma Hatch just made up another bed on the couch, and Aunt Goldie joined our temporary household by sleeping straight through twenty-four hours.

Later, when her memory improved somewhat, Goldie told us she vaguely remembered fleeing from Meves with a trucker who had headed his rig east on I-80, promising to get her to safety. True to his word, he took her to a safe place. That it was 150 miles down the road was a bafflement to all of us.

During the next few weeks, all that the people in Grand Island could talk about was Black Tuesday. "Did you get hit?" became the official greeting on the street, and "Would you believe—?" was the surest way to get a conversation started. Everyone had a story to tell.

There was also no end to the comparing going on. After the official investigation, our storm was labeled a first-class freak. The six or seven funnels that touched down didn't follow tornado rules at all. Not for size, direction, or velocity. Most tornadoes are less than half a mile wide. Wouldn't you know the one menacing the countryside near Phillips reached five miles in width? And in spite of the fact that

99.5 percent of Northern Hemisphere tornadoes turn counterclockwise, two of ours spun the other way. Even Dr. Fujita, the great tornado wizard, was baffled.

"I've never seen anything like it in my twenty-seven years of tornado investigating," he said in the Grand Island *Daily Independent.* "I've never seen such a complicated tornado."

I was hearing something else as the days went by, something that proved itself true again and again: "What happens *after* a tornado is the real story." If you'd been in south-central Nebraska last summer, you'd have to agree.

What do you do, for instance, when the city's water supply is polluted, when you aren't allowed to drink what isn't in the pipes, even if you had a faucet to turn it on? Morning, noon, and night we guzzled root beer, Pepsi, the un-cola drink, or Dr Pepper. Whatever we could get. I never thought I'd get sick of drinking soda pop, but I did.

Furthermore, what do you do when you don't have clothes to wear except the ones on your back, food to eat, or a place to go to the bathroom? Things can get hairy! You find yourself swapping a perfectly good wristwatch you found in the trash heap for a candy bar because you need the energy. Then the girl with the watch swaps it for a T-shirt that's cleaner than the one she's wearing.

After a couple of days, the meat begins to rot and stink in the grocery stores because there's no electricity. Strange dogs and horses start hanging around—who need food and water as much as you do. By and by there's talk of looters coming in at night to steal whatever's left. And every day, with the humidity soaring and the hot sun beating down, you wonder how you'll get rid of the tons and tons of debris piling up everywhere.

Like Dad said, you just raise up your head and yell, "Help!"

That's when the miracle happens.

Suddenly, *everyone* became our neighbor. The National Guard, REACT, the Red Cross, volunteers whose own homes had been untouched. Neighbors were coming out of the woodwork, as the saying goes. The Mennonites arrived in droves, rolled up their sleeves, and dug in. A disaster team from as far away as Wichita Falls, Texas, showed up without having to be asked. One ancient farmer brought fifteen milk cans full of water all the way from Broken Bow, Nebraska—every noon!—in heat you wouldn't believe, so people could quench their thirst.

In our own neighborhood, Mrs. Smiley was the

shining example. She got the Mennonites to move her two big tables out on the grass, then conned those young men into passing eighty-seven jars of canned goods through the basement window. Every day she served applesauce, plums, cherries, and luke-warm stewed tomatoes to anyone who needed to eat. (In flowered paper cups yet!)

Mrs. Smiley's "open house," which really was open to the sky, became a neighborhood gathering place. It was great to lie there in the shade of her cotton-woods for a minute when you needed to rest and gather your wits. Arthur and I and our dads did it several times.

No wonder the Presbyterian men's club turned out full force that next weekend to start Mrs. Smiley's new roof.

To tell you the truth, though, what tickled her most was having Arthur and me return her old screen door. Arthur found it unharmed exactly where he'd stashed it in his basement. With one of us at each end, we carried it from his place to hers.

"It'll look wonderful on my new back porch!" Mrs. Smiley chortled gleefully, greeting the colorful patches like old friends. "I'm so glad you saved it for me!"

Even the President of the United States dropped

by to see us mopping up. Even *he* became our neighbor!

"You won't be forgotten," promised Jimmy Carter, speaking from a foundation in the midst of our Sand Crane rubble. And we weren't. By the middle of August, Arthur's family had a government-issued trailer to live in—rent free. A week later, ours arrived. Up and down the street, hookups were installed and families moved back to their properties.

By the time school started, our neighborhood looked like trailer town, for sure. Mom's only complaint was that Ryan couldn't make it through his nap for all the hammering and sawing going on outside.

Now an entire year has passed since that black-letter day in June. I've gone through four inner tubes on the new Voyageur Grandpa bought me. I also finished the seventh grade in that period of time and got an *A* on my science project. It wasn't easy, but I managed to demonstrate how radical changes in atmospheric pressure can cause sucking sounds in a person's drainpipes.

Tonight, June 3, we're having an anniversary party here in our new house. Almost everybody in Grand Island is celebrating, as a matter of fact. KHAS-TV is going to rerun the hour-long documentary they made of our disaster, so several neighbors are coming for potluck. Afterward we'll watch the show together.

"And give thanks," Grandma reminds me.

The Darlingtons are coming, of course. In fact, Arthur's already here, having offered to come early. "In case you need me," he said. What he's doing is setting up card tables while I tend Ryan. (Keeping Ryan away from Minerva II is no small assignment, you understand. Picture a circus bear, arms outstretched, swaying from side to side. That's Ryan, aged one and a half, chasing the cat.)

From the front window here, I can see Stacey coming down the street pushing Tempest June, girl number seven, in a stroller. My heart skips a beat, the way it always does when I see Stacey.

The person we're all going to miss tonight is Mrs. Smiley. She didn't make it all the way to the anniversary. She was sitting in the doctor's office one day in March, just waiting for an appointment. She hadn't been feeling too spry, she had told Mom earlier.

"I guess her dear old heart simply quit beating," Mom said that night.

It's my opinion that her heart was too big to be

housed in such an insignificant body. You can't put a 6.6-liter engine in a little old compact and not expect something to blow.

I was truly sorry she couldn't have been a spectator at the fine funeral the Presbyterians gave her that Sunday morning. Everyone in the neighborhood, even the Catholics who generally went to Mass, attended her final open house. It was the kind of farewell Mrs. Smiley would have loved.

Now, out in the kitchen, Mom and Aunt Goldie are making enough coleslaw to feed the entire National Guard.

"Doesn't it need something?" I hear Aunt Goldie ask. "More salt or vinegar or—"

"It's perfect!" Mom answers her like an older sister. "Just mix it, would you?"

In the dining room, Grandma Hatch, an apron over her lavender birthday dress, is setting the table with our new dishes.

Naturally, Grandpa's out in the garage with Dad. Restoring the Corvette has become their #1 project, now that the house is finished.

I can smell coffee coming from the big twenty-four-cup urn Mom borrowed from the Millers, so I know I'll soon be asked to help with something. Sure enough, over Ryan's gurgly laugh (on capturing the